Green Ivy Publishing
1 Lincoln Centre
18W140 Butterfield Road
Suite 1500
Oakbrook Terrace IL 60181-4843
www.greenivybooks.com

ISBN: 978-1-944680-76-3

Letters to Jessie

Patricia Pulver Fitzgerald

Chapter 1

Jessie Alberta Whitney was born in Burlington, Washington, on August 7, 1896, to Anna Rose Dunnet Whitney and William Hiram Whitney. Her father was a farmer at that time, though he would later serve as Burlington city treasurer, county assessor, county treasurer, and a member of the school board of directors. Her mother, Anna Rose, cared for Jessie and her three older siblings, Irene, Margaret (Etta), and William (Bill). Those four were later joined by a younger sister, Rosamond, and Ernest, who did not survive past early childhood.

From left William, Anna Rose holding Ernest, Margaret (Etta), Irene (in back), William holding Jessie. Ernest did not live long after this photo, and Rosamond was born several years after this photo was taken.

Jessie lived in a time when, as in much of our history, correspondence was done through letters delivered by the postal service. The only thing remarkable about Jessie's letters was that she saved almost two hundred of them. They spanned six generations, beginning with letters of advice from her grandmother and ending with affectionate notes from her great-grandchildren. We'll begin with a look at Jessie's letters from her grandmother, Jane Dunnet.

Jane Dunnet was born Jane Forsyth, on October 15, 1840, in Northesk, New Brunswick, Canada. She lived her entire life within a few miles of Northesk but visited her daughter, Anna Rose Dunnet, in Burlington, Washington, for a year. Jane was widowed at forty-seven years of age, before Jessie was born. According to the 1911 Canadian census, at that time she lived with her son Edward, his wife, Mary, and their four children in North Esk. She wrote letters or postcards to Jessie when she was a child. Jane Dunnet continued to write after Jessie grew up and had children of her own.

Jane Forsyth Dunnet

Dear Jessie, How are you living? Hope you are well. We are having very cold weather. Is Etta staying home or does she work out? She might write to me sometime. Do you go to school or help mama? Would like to hear from you sometime. Yours lovingly, Grandma

This is one of the earlier postcards Jessie received from her grandmother. Her plea that Etta "might write to me sometime" is an oft-repeated comment, not only by their grandmother but, later, by their Aunt Margaret, who was a regular correspondent as well. Apparently, Jessie's sister Etta was not a frequent letter writer. Jane Dunnet also entreated Jessie to get her mother (Jane's daughter) to write more frequently.

Jane spent a year in Burlington when Jessie was twelve years old and Irene was eighteen. During this time, Irene received a letter from Jane's daughter, Margaret, who was Irene and Jessie's aunt.

You are all so kind to Grandma there that I suppose she will not come back. If she does not come back when her year is up, I will have to go there for her, and then you will have two of us to bother with. She writes of having such a good time. Some of these days I will send you my photo if you would care to have it. I look very sober, but I have lots of things to make me look like that. I lead a very busy life, and have many worries. It is wash-day, and I should be in the kitchen looking after the wash-woman. She does very well, anyway. But I am a poor boss.

In 1907 Jane wrote a letter to Jessie's sister Irene, telling her that she had been sick.

I will soon be able to be around again. I sent to town today for some beef iron and wine. It is a great medicine to give a person strength.

One must wonder if she mixed these, or did she just drink the wine separately?

Castle Street, Newcastle, N.B.

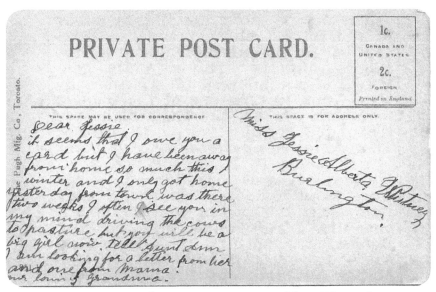

Dear Jessie, It seems that I owe you a card but I have been away from home so much this winter and I only got home yesterday from town, was there two weeks. I often see you in my mind driving the cows to pasture but you will be a big girl now. Tell Aunt Ann I am looking for a letter from her and one from Mama. Your loving grandma

The Aunt Ann mentioned here was Annie (or Anna) Rogers, Jane's sister, who had also moved to Burlington. She was a widow at this time and owned her own home according to the 1910 census. Anna was involved in the local Baptist church, of which she was an original member. Numerous newspaper articles, published in the *Bellingham Herald* but covering social life in Burlington, mentioned Anna Rogers, the name Annie used at that time. It seems to have been common practice to interchange the names Ann, Anna, and Annie, making it more confusing, especially since many members of this family had these names.

Tuesday evening the old members of the Baptist church tendered a reception to the new members in the Baptist church. The program consisted of an address of welcome by Mrs. Anna Rogers, one of the pioneer members of the church, which was responded to by Mr. A. D. Fraser, Then followed addresses by Mrs. Bishop, of Kent; R. M. Moody and J. A. Walker. Several very pretty songs were sung and ice cream and cake was served. Those present were: Mr. and Mrs. J. A. Walker, Mr. and Mrs. Dennis, Mr. and Mrs. M. LaMar, Mrs. Anna Rogers, Mr. and Mrs. Oscar Mapes, Mr. and Mrs. Fred Marchant, Mr. and Mrs. Ed Darcy, Mr. and Mrs. Burch, Mr. and Mrs. Charles Fringer, Mr. and Mrs. Pearl Fringer, Mr. and Mrs. James Crossley, Mr. and Mrs. Roy Moody, Mr. and Mrs. A. D. Fraser, Dr. and Mrs. I. B. Shoemaker, Mrs. Lester Smith, Mrs. S. L. Moody, Mrs. William Whitney, Mrs. Owen Fulk, Mrs. Martin, Mrs. Healey, Mrs. Hoover, Mrs. Bishop, of Kent; Mrs. Pauline Thomas, Mrs. George Cressy and daughter, Rose, of Seattle; Miss Ina Williams, Miss Mattie LaMar, Miss Leah Dennis, Misses Maxie and Nellie Marchant, Miss Etta Whitney, Misses Eva and Iris Shoemaker, Miss Demull, Misses Lottie, Vela and Wanda Fulk, Miss Grace Healey, Mr. W. T. Elmore, Mr. Francis Healey, Mr. Arlo Fulk, Mr. Louis LaMor, Mr. H. M. Moody, Dr. Hunt, Mr. A. J. Stacey

Jessie's mother, Mrs. William Whitney, was at that meeting

too, as was Jessie's sister Etta.

Dear Jessie got your card and many thanks. Glad to hear that you are all well. Tell mama that my address is the same. She don't write now. Do you still go to school? Love to everybody. Good-bye, Grandma

This is the house, on Rio Vista Street in Burlington, where Jessie lived as a child. After her husband, Rudolph, died she moved back to care for her elderly father, William Hiram Whitney, and she remained there after his death. The house is, to this day, much as it was then, but there are now houses surrounding it, and trees and shrubs partially obscure it from view. Jessie's grandchildren spent many happy days there and often spent the night, usually sleeping in the upstairs room on the right.

Jessie married Rudolph Henry Pulver, on September 4, 1915, when she was nineteen years old and a 1914 graduate of Burlington High School. She and Rude, as she always called him, had an eleven-year age difference. He was thirty years old and an established farmer when they married. A letter, written February 6, 1916, was received from her grandmother shortly after their marriage and before children came along.

Jessie and Rudolph's wedding picture

Whitneyville, Feb, 6th

Dear Jessie,

received your both letters was glad to hear from you. hope you wont forget to write sometime for I really think your mother had forgotten me altogether I think her last letter was dated the last of November and that seems to be a long time for her it makes me worrie when I dont get a letter from her am afraid she or some of the rest of the family are sick I sent her a post card last week hope she got it all right am sending her the present of the Leader for a year. she will have the second one by the time you get this letter.

Dear Jessie, received your... letters, was glad to hear from you. Hope you won't forget to write sometime for I really think your mother has forgotten me altogether. I think her last letter was dated the last of November and that seems to be a long time for her. It makes me worrie when I don't get a letter from her am afraid she or some of the rest of the family are sick. I sent her a post card last week, hope she got it all right. Am sending her the present of the Leader for a year. She will have the second one by the time you get this letter.

2   *after*

[handwritten letter reproduced in print below]

I don't suppose you see her very often now you have a house of your own now to look after and a man to cook for but I know he is awful nice or you wouldn't have anything to do with him. Don't tell him, he will think I am flattering him.

I am sure you must have been surprised to see that fall of snow that came for you don't have storms like that out there. Those that had sleighs would enjoy a drive. That is more snow than we have had yet this winter. We have had a lovely winter so far and not much frost I think. The climates are changing all over the world and this terrible war will it ever cease?

Canada had officially declared war on Germany on August 5, 1914, so they had seen more than two years of war at this time, and Canadian casualties were high. By the end, Canadian troops had seen 39 percent casualties. (Wikipedia)

This is the Pulver family that Jessie married into. Her husband, Rudolph, is the first man on the left in the back row. His brothers are, from left: Fred, Frank, Peter, and Edward, seated by their father, also named Rudolph. The girls are Anna, seated next to her mother, also named Anna, and Lena and Mern in the back row. The parents had emigrated from Switzerland and were farmers in the Skagit Valley.

(3)   until

[Handwritten text transcribed below]

Some of our dear boys from Loggie has been killed and some from
Campbelton not far from here. When we get the papers, the first thing
I look for is the casualties. There are about two hundred training now
in Newcastle, will leave here in March. So many young fellows 16 and
17 years old. They don't know what they have to face yet, it is only
play now.

Your Uncle Ed is not very well just now, he has the grippe and Kathleen hasn't been down stairs for three days until this afternoon. She
has grippe too. It has carried off a lot of old people this winter and
indeed young people too. I am thankful I have escaped so far.

Well dear, I don't know as I have anything to write to interest you? I wish I was near enough to you to run in and get some of your cooking. I know it would be good. I do hope dear Irene will continue better for there is nothing like health in this world. Money can't buy it.

So now take good care of yourself and don't lift things that is heavy. I am just giving you a grandma's advice. Don't be offended dear.

Kind regards to your husband, and write when convenient. Will be glad to hear from you at any time. Your loving grandma, Jane Dunnet

The reference to not lifting heavy things indicates that Jane Dunnet knew that Jessie was pregnant. However, in her letters to Jessie during her pregnancies, this condition was not referred to directly as a pregnancy but as "troubles."

Jane Dunnet indicated she was in Whitneyville when this letter was written. She said the next one was from Red Bank, but it was postmarked Sunny Corner. Sunny Corner and Red Bank are both on the Miramichi River, about twelve miles from the current town of Miramichi, but they are on opposite sides of the river. Whitneyville does not appear on modern day maps, but Whitney is there, near North Esk and South Esk and also near Miramichi. Miramichi is made up of Newcastle, Loggieville, and other small communities and was established in 1995.

Sickness and injury were a big part of life in the early 1900's in rural Canada. In this next letter, Jane Dunnet gives an account of both. She discusses three of Anna Rose's siblings, Edward, Margaret, and Marjorie. They all lived near one another. In the early 1900's, when young people moved across the continent to start a new life, they were unlikely to see their siblings again. Margaret, however, did go to visit Anna Rose in Burlington on two occasions.

Jane Dunnet's three eldest children are pictured below. They are Edward, Anna Rose, and Margaret Jane, who is seated.

Dear Jessie, Your very kind and welcome letter was received some time ago, was glad to hear that you were all well. I had a letter from your mother shortly after I got yours. Thought I would answer her letter first. I was glad to hear that Irene was keeping better. Hope she may keep better. The warm weather will help her. I have been up to your Aunt Marjorie's for the last three weeks. They are all well down home. I was talking to your Uncle Ed a few days ago over the phone. Your Aunt Margaret is better and she was able to teach again.

Jane refers to Jessie's sister Irene being sick. Irene was suffering from tuberculosis, which would soon claim her life. She was initially treated at home but was later sent to a sanitarium. Irene sent this postcard to Jessie, on July 29, 1916, from Orting, Washington. She wrote only three sentences: *"Will be home soon. Why don't you write me a letter? Don't write now though. Irene."*

(2)

She had a bad attack of pleurisy and was out of school two weeks.

We are having cold backward now. Our ice isn't out of the (river) yet. The wheeling is very poor. The people are all busy cutting their wood. Gasoline machines everywhere and accidents happening, too. Adam Hill's son, Tom, had part of his hand taken off on Thursday. They took him to the hospital. The doctors think they will save his hand or part of it. Your mother knows who they are. Perlie's oldest son, Weldon, had his arm badly cut too two weeks ago yesterday.

"Wheeling" most likely refers to getting around in a wheeled vehicle. According to *Webster's Dictionary*, wheeling is "the condition of a road for travel by wheeled vehicles."

(3)

They took him right to the doctor...and he put seven stitches in it. So many accidents happening.

I suppose your husband has most of his farming done. We are always late here farming. Our seasons are late.

Well, dear, I am going to have a little confidential talk with you.

How are you keeping? Hope you are real well and not working too hard. You must be careful and not lift too much and be careful, dear, and eat too much meat for that is not good for anyone in your condition. It isn't good for the kidneys but I suppose you (know) without me telling you.

Jane freely gave advice to Jessie during her pregnancy and, in this case, warned her of eating too much meat because of the harm it could do to her kidneys. She continues to refer to Jessie's "trouble" instead of her pregnancy.

I wish I was near, dear, so I could help you out of your trouble, but then you will have your dear mother with you and your husband's mother if she is living. Some of you must write as soon as all is over and let me know.

If you see your mother soon tell (her) that Bessie Whitney was married this week and went on her marriage tour this week to Truro. She married Melvin Stewart tell her, a son of David Stewart. His mother was Agnes Mutch. It was a surprise to everyone. Well dear, I will close for this time; will be pleased to hear from you when you feel like writing.

Kind regards to your husband and a good share to yourself. Yours lovingly, Grandma

This letter will likely be opened before you get it for our letters coming from the states are opened and closed again. I don't know why.

The envelope shows evidence of the censorship of letters to and from Canada and the US during World War 1.

Dear Jessie, you don't know how glad I was to hear that you were over your trouble, for it is something that worries a person a lot until it is over. You didn't say what you were going to name her but I suppose it will be a great big name. I wish I was near enough to take the little dear in my arms and hug her. I suppose your mama feels quite old now being a grandma. I am looking for a letter from her for the last three weeks. I have been in town for three weeks just got home two days ago. Was nursing a doctor's wife.

The baby had been born May 5, 1916, and was named Anna June; she was always called June.

(2.)

a trained nurse and he called me up over the phone and then sent a rig after me but we got along fine he gave me a compliment he said I done just as well as a trained nurse could do. how is Irene doing hope she is all right by this time poor girl it seems too bad and her so young we are having cold back ward weather here now no farming done yet to speak of your uncle Ed is getting ready to fish he is driving picketts we will be glad to get some fresh fish for people tires on so much meat isent this a terrible war your cousin Hearld is in England now he will soon

He couldn't get a trained nurse and he called me up over the phone and then sent a rig after me but we got along fine. He gave me a compliment. He said I done just as well as a trained nurse could do.

How is Irene doing? Hope she is alright by this time poor girl. It seems too bad and her so young. We are having cold backward weather here now so no farming done yet to speak of. Your Uncle Ed is getting ready to fish. He is driving picketts. We will be glad to get some fresh fish for people tires on so much meat.

Isn't this a terrible war? Your cousin, Hearld is in England now.

The cousin that Jane refers to, Hearld, may be Harold Whitney, son of William Hiram's brother, Fredrick H. Whitney. He was Jessie's cousin and would have been just two years older than Jessie, about the right age to be fighting in World War I.

Jane apparently made a living by doing nursing, in people's homes, when they needed full-time care for sick or injured family members. In fact, her comment about wishing she could help Jessie with her trouble indicates she was a midwife. There are other references elsewhere that suggest this also.

He will soon be going to France to fight in the trenches. I hope he will come home safe, poor boy. He is an only son.

Well dear, if I had got your letter while I was in town I would have got a few snap shots, but I suppose it would scare you, but if I am spared to go to town again I will get some. Now this is only a few lines at this time. Will write more next time I write. Tell your husband not to be too proud of this baby and not spoil her. They all join in love to you and wishing you happiness with your dear little girl. Tell mama to write. Your loving grandma, Jane Dunnet

Dear Jessie, Your long looked for letter came to hand yesterday, was very much pleased to get it, also, the pictures. I am very proud of my great-granddaughter, would love to hold her in my arms, the dear baby. But Jessie, don't think too much of her. We have no lease of their lives. My first three, when the oldest was four, and the little girl two and the baby one month old all died in eleven days' time from the first one died until the last one was buried. The little girl was a treasure, and we made too much of her.

She could say every word as plain as we could. We were left without any, but that dread disease diphtheria took them all with lots of other dear ones. But that isn't saying, dear, that your little girl is going to die for indeed she looks well alive, but you know what I mean. I know you won't take amiss at anything I say. She is the picture of health and if it won't make you proud, she is very pretty. Tell your husband that I think she looks like him for I know he is good looking.

Well dear, I want to thank you both for thinking of me at all. I am very proud of that picture and will get it set in a nice little frame the first time I go to town.

I had a letter today from your mother. She feels badly over poor Irene's case and so do I feel sorry for her, poor dear girl. I hope the doctors in Portland will be able to cure her. There is nothing like health, money can't buy it.

I wish we lived nearer to each other. It is so far to send a little parcel.

I am feeling fairly well with the exception of my head and it troubles me a lot. I take spells of sneezing and will sneeze a whole day. I have tried three doctors and spent so much money this last year and got no cure. But oh I am getting old. I can't expect to be always well. I have a case coming off most any day now.

One can only imagine the pain it must have caused Jane to write of the deaths of her three children so many years before. One must also wonder what it was like for Jessie to read about this loss as she held her infant daughter in her arms. Life was very fragile for children in the 1860's, and death was always a threat. Diphtheria was one of the major causes of childhood death, at that time, and sometimes took all the children in a family. It is a respiratory disease caused by bacteria, but since the advent of widespread immunization of children, it has become rare in most developed countries.

Jane talks about Jessie's sister Irene, who was in Portland. Irene suffered from tuberculosis and had been sent to a sanitarium there in hopes of a cure.

I tried to persuade her to get a trained nurse but she pleaded so hard I had to promise her. We have no experienced nurses around and the trained ones charges from fifteen to twenty dollars a week. I had six applications for the winter the last to come off the first of April but I refused them all but two. Well dear, you will be tired reading this scribbling. My hand shakes now. Wishing you all a very merry Christmas and a happy New Year and many returns of them. I remain your loving grandma, Jane Dunnet

Please write soon. A kiss for baby, and give me Irene's address.

Dear Jessie,

Received your welcome letter a week ago. It must have been detained – it was dated sixteen days before I got it so I thought I would try and scribble you a few lines although it is quite an effort. I have been very sick for the last two weeks but am improving slowly, a heavy cold and throat trouble. Measles is very bad around here but we had them years ago. I guess Mama remembers all about it. She was very sick with them too.

Now dear, I want you to overlook all mistakes and poor scribbling for my hand shakes a lot today. Well, I was glad to hear from all. Sorry to hear that dear little June had whooping cough. Hope she will soon be better. There is a lot of whooping cough around here this spring too, especially at Red Bank.

The delay in receiving the letter was most likely caused by World War I's effect on Canada. Jane was seventy-six at the time she wrote this letter, and she had begun to write more about her frailties. She lived just one more year after this letter was written.

Whooping cough was another disease that had to be reckoned with, and June was still a baby when she had it.

We are having terrible weather here now. Snow, slush, and rain. It is as cold today as it was in March. The ice went out two days ago, and we are expecting the Steamboat up this afternoon to be ready to take her regular trips Monday morning.

I have been looking for a letter from your mother for some time. I may get one today. I get lonesome when I don't hear from her. I wrote to Etta some time ago, hope she got it all right. I asked her for a photo of her and her husband. I may hear from her soon.

Well dear, I am sorry to hear that you are in trouble so soon again, but the hotter the war, the sooner peace. They will all grow up together. Tell Rude he has to do better than that in the future.

Jane was not shy about giving advice, including raising the topic of birth control, as indicated in the last sentence on this page, and she put that responsibility on the husband. She was also outspoken about opposing a pregnancy so soon after the first baby was born.

Jane Dunnet

(3) I suppose you go to see Mama quite often. Go as often as you can for you may not always have mama to go and see. It is a great thing to have a mother and she must be lonesome for poor Irene for she was a lovely girl. I trust she is better off than battling with this miserable sinful world.

I suppose you go to see Mama quite often. Go as often as you can for you may not always have mama to go and see. It is a great thing to have a mother and she must be lonesome for poor Irene for she was a lovely girl. I trust she is better off than battling with this miserable sinful world.

Well, Jessie dear, I have nothing to interest you. Wish I was near enough to go and see you all. Uncle Robert's two little boys have had measles very bad, but are better now. Claire and Nelson.

If you see Mama, give her my love and tell her that Annie Gills (?) third son is killed in the war. Willie John...

...he was about twenty years old, a splendid young fellow. Am not able to write any more today, will do better next time I hope. Kind regards to your husband and a kiss for dear little June.

Your loving grandma, Jane Dunnet

Measles was another threat to the health of young children in the early years of the twentieth century. The two boys mentioned were Jessie's first cousins, whom she probably never met.

Dear Jessie, You will begin to think that I have forgotten you, but not at all. After I got better and able to go around I went to town and stayed ten days and came home yesterday and am feeling pretty strong. I think the visit done me good. Next week I will go up to your Aunt Marjorie's for a month for I am at home there.

We are having very warm weather here now and the crops were late going in but they are coming in lovely now. The wheat and potatoes are great. I hope the wheat will be good so we can have flour of our own for it is fifteen dollars a barrel now. I do wish the war was over for it is a terrible war. Has Willie enlisted yet? We have conscription.

Marjorie was Jane's youngest living child and the ninth of ten born to her. Marjorie was born in 1878 when Jane was thirty-eight and Jessie's mother, Anna Rose, was eight years old. Marjorie was just eleven years old when Anna Rose married and left home.

Willie was Jessie's older brother, William, and he did serve in World War I.

Willie, Anna Rose, Etta, Jessie, Rosamond, William

I am in hopes that it will soon be over. Hope your husband won't have to go. There are wives in our town that has five and six children and their husbands go. It must be a hard parting. Dear little June looks lovely in her picture. I am sorry her nose will be broken so soon but the hotter war the sooner peace. Be careful, dear, and don't work too hard nor lift heavy things for there are three or four women around here that are invalids from that.

Your Aunt Margaret leaves the fourth for Halifax to have her eyes tested. She will be away four weeks at the least.

I do wish I lived within two or three hundred miles of your mother and the rest of you. I would see you all before the snow flies again. I do hope that your mama will be able to come next summer and that I may live to meet her once more. Tell her that Uncle Ed wishes she was near to get some salmon and grilts. The fish are very plen-

tiful this summer. They have about sixty barrels of gaspereau salted away now. Of course they sell them to the fish merchants.

Well, dear, I think I will close for this time. I have nothing to write to interest you. Will be pleased to hear from you at any time that you feel like writing.

Kind regards to your husband and a kiss and hug for dear little Annie June. Your loving grandma, Jane Dunnet

Breakfast baking is thirty-five cents a pound, expensive eating.

When Jane said she was sorry June's nose would be broken soon, it seems to be a saying similar to the modern expression that someone's nose is "out of joint." It means someone feels ill-treated or thinks someone else is receiving preferential treatment. In this case, June would be adapting to a new baby. Once again Jane gave advice about not lifting heavy things, but this time she gave an example of three or four women nearby who were invalids because of doing just that. One wonders how Jessie took this advice, by ceasing to lift heavy items, or with an eye roll.

Many people along the Miramichi River, where the Dunnets lived, made their living by farming, logging, or fishing. Canadians were encouraged to eat more fish during the war so that the soldiers and allies could have meat. They were also asked to eat less wheat, beans, and dairy products, substituting fish, cereals made from other grains, fruits, and vegetables. Food became expensive during the war. The gaspereau Jane referred to are a salt-water fish.

Dear Jessie, You don't know how pleased I was to get your letter and to hear that you were so well over your trouble and had a nice boy. One more and stop then, that will be a nice family.

I have been away for a week in Littleton. Your mother knows the place. This woman was Edward Tozer's daughter. Her husband came for me with his car. I stayed ten days and came home this morning. Her dear little baby is deformed, has two reel feet and a growth on its back. It was hard on my nerves to dress the dear child. Its mother is real smart and was up and dressed when I left. I don't think it can live over a day or two more.

Jessie's baby boy was born August 2, 1917, and was named William Rudolph Pulver. He changed it to William Whitney Pulver around the time he graduated from high school.

Again Jane had advice for her granddaughter regarding family planning. She suggested that they have just one more child even though she had given birth to ten and knew how fragile the life of a child could be then.

Jessie and William Pulver

Spinal (that isn't spelled right) meningitis has set in and it can't live more than a day or two.

Aunt Margaret has gone back to her school again. Her school isn't as large as it was last term.

We are having lovely harvest here now, our wheat is ready to cut, our potatoes are lovely, both large and dry.

If this war would only come to an end what a blessing it would be. There are predictions it will be over about Christmas. Everything is a terrible price now. Print that we got for twelve cents is eighteen cents now.

Well Jessie, what is the trouble with Etta? She has never written me a line. I would like to get her picture with her husband. I have the rest of your photos. I don't know her reason for not writing.

Jane mentioned again the high prices of goods in Canada during the war, and she stated it should be over by Christmas. As we know, it ended on November 11, 1918, nearly a year later.

I am sure I forgot to tell you that your mother sent me a card when your baby was born, but I haven't had a letter from her since the last of June.

Where is Willie? Has he gone to the war or is he home?

Well you have named the baby. It was nice to call it for your Father. I got your mama's and little June's picture when I got home this morning. It is lovely. Your mama looks fine.

Well dear, I have nothing to write to interest you. Will be glad to hear from you at any time. Tell mama when you see her to try and write me once more. I get lonesome when I don't hear from her. Good-by and kiss those babies for me. Kind regards to your husband. Lovingly, Grandma

Anna Rose, apparently, was still remiss in writing to her mother. With letters being virtually the only method of correspondence at that time, they had such importance.

Dear Jessie, You don't know how pleased I was to get that snap shot of you and the baby. Isn't he a darling, and do you know I can see his grandpa's looks in him across the eyes. I don't want to make you proud, but I think he is very pretty. Hope the dear boy may be spared to you all.

Well Jessie, I have had a terrible time after the fall I got, just getting better by degrees, but am in hopes I will be all right again. My right side hurts me a lot yet.

Well Jessie, the war still goes on. Lots of our boys have been examined and will have to go when called on. Too bad if Willie has to go.

The lines about the new baby carry her subtle warnings about caring too much for the child because something bad could happen. Jane knew, from experience, how tenuous the life of a child could be. She had lost her first three children in 1865, and a two-year-old son, Ingraham, in 1884.

Jane continued to express concern for her grandson, Willie, asking whether he would have to serve in the war.

The only boy too, but we will have to put up with it.

Well dear, I don't know as you will be able to read this, my hand shakes so, but make it out if you can.

We are having lovely weather here now, scarcely any frost yet, but two weeks ago we had a terrible wind storm, blowed down great big trees, broke down telephone wires and posts for miles up and down the river. No communications with the central for two days and nights. It was a terrible night. There is a grove back of our house – your mother knows it – broke the trees off like pipe stems, lots of people didn't sleep a wink all night. However next morning was lovely.

The price of everything still keeps up although potatoes are selling in town for three dollars now, but people think they will be four before spring. Butter still keeps up and for eggs they can't get them for love nor money.

Tell mama I am looking for a letter from her soon. I get lonesome when I don't hear from her. I know she has a lot to do and her alone. I can't see what has happened to Etta. I think I always answered her letters when she used to write.

Diphtheria has broken out in Newcastle. They may have to close the schools and opera houses. There is one case of smallpox too in town.

Well, I don't think I have anything to interest you and will close. You write so faithfully. I cannot expect you to write so often and you with two children.

Do not neglect your darling babies to write, just when you have a good chance write. I am always glad to get your nice bright letters. Remember me kindly to your beloved husband. Tell him no more babies for three years at the least. Ha ha! Kiss the babies for me.

Love to them all at home. Your loving grandma, Jane Dunnet

One wonders how Jessie's husband, Rude, reacted to the continuing unsolicited family planning advice, or if Jessie even passed those messages on to him.

Dear Jessie, Your kind and welcome (letter) received yesterday. I didn't get your other one answered. Many, many thanks to you dear for your kind remembrances of me. Came the day after my birthday. It was so thoughtful of you to remember me and me so far away. I can only write a short letter today. It gives me all I can do to sit and write. A week ago today I was going out at our back door and it was raining and my two feet went from under me and I fell right on my back and was hurt all over. I have been in bed most ever since, but I am not suffering much pain today.

Our folks finished digging only about sixty barrels, but we ought to be thankful for that many for some didn't have their seed.

Hope them dear babies are well and will keep well. Kiss them both for me for I never expect to see them.

Kind regards to your husband and tell him I don't want to hear tell of any more babies for four years.

I can't sit any longer, will write a longer letter next time. My back pains so bad.

Your loving grandma, Jane Dunnet

Will be pleased to hear from you when you have time to write for you must be very busy.

In the previous letter, Jane said that Jessie and Rude should wait three years before having another child, and now she said they should wait four years. It turned out that June and William were the only two they had.

Chapter 2

The next letters are addressed to Jessie at the Portland Open Air Sanatorium in Milwaukie, Oregon where she had been sent, in hopes of a cure for tuberculosis, in 1918. These may have been the last two letters to Jessie from her grandmother. Jane died before the warm days of summer that year. Jessie recovered and lived many more years.

The Portland Open Air Sanatorium was advertised this way in the 1924 *Polk's Portland City Directory*:

A Thoroughly Up-to-date Institution for the Modern Scientific Treatment of Tuberculosis

Location *Six miles south of Portland in a grove of fir and cedar on a rock bluff towering 300 feet above the Willamette River, commanding a picturesque view of the river, city and surrounding mountains.*

Object *The exclusive treatment of tuberculosis by the careful application of the most modern physical, dietetic, hygienic and specific procedures.*

Advantages *Artificial Penumothorax and Tuberculin in suitable cases: X-ray and Laboratory facilities. Individual Cottages with steam heated dressing rooms, hot and cold running water and shower and tub baths. Trained Nurses. Certified milk from tuberculin tested herd.*

Tuberculosis is an infectious lung disease, and over half of the people contracting it die if left untreated.

Before the development of antibiotics to treat pneumonia, doctors recommended sanitariums for those fortunate enough to get into the limited spaces there. If that was not an option, patients were treated with "fresh air and plenty of food," according to an article by D. H. Bernstein in the *Canadian Medical Association Journal* from January 1918.

My dear Jessie, I received your welcome letter, but oh so sorry to hear that you were poorly, but I some expected to hear that you were poorly. I had a presentiment that you were going to have a sick spell for that grippe is a hard thing to grapple with, but oh my dear do take good care of yourself.

Look Jessie, do you like buttermilk? If you do, try and get it and drink all you can or all you want that is if your doctor approves of it.

Our doctor recommends it highly. Elese Hare has a daughter that has been sick all winter. She took pneumonia and pleurisy and the doctor at Red Bank didn't treat her right so they got another doctor, Doctor Dissmond, and he told her to drink all the buttermilk she could. I do think it saved your mother's life when she was a girl and came home from Boston sick. I have been dreaming so much this winter about you all. I have been looking for a letter from your mother for a month and have got none...

Jane Dunnet, who had cared for others who were sick and needed her, was now unable to help her beloved granddaughter.

3

so I went to work the other day and wrote to her. I suppose the poor girl is worried about you and then she has the dear little baby to attend, but look dear, don't you worrie or fret any more than you can help. I hope you will be all right again. I will pray for you every day I live and as soon as I get a letter from your mother I will write to her every week and hear from you and look dear, don't write to me without you feel yourself getting stronger, but I do love to get your letters, so be sure and keep Jolly.

During Jessie's stay at the sanitarium her parents, the Whitneys, took care of baby Billy, and Rude's parents, the Pulvers, cared for June, who was a toddler at that time. Jane's sadness about Jessie's illness is palpable in these words. She seemed to have no illusion about the danger, having lost Jessie's sister Irene to the same disease just months earlier.

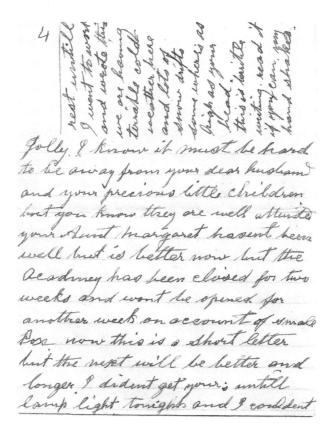

I know it must be hard to be away from your dear husband and your precious little children but you know they are well attended.

Your Aunt Margaret hasn't been well, but is better now, but the Academy has been closed for two weeks and won't be opened for another week on account of smallpox.

Now this is a short letter but the next will be better and longer. I didn't get yours until lamplight tonight and I couldn't rest until I went to work and wrote this. We are having terrible cold weather here and lots of snow drifts. Somewhere's as high as your head. This is terrible writing. Read it if you can. My hand shakes. Kind love to your dear husband, and tell him to look on the sunny side at all times. Your loving grandma, Jane Dunnet

Sickness and disease played a large part in the lives of people in rural Canada in the early years of the twentieth century. A school closure of three weeks for smallpox would be unheard of in our times. The Spanish flu epidemic would also come later that year, 1918.

Dear Jessie, Received your kind and ever welcome letter. Was so glad to hear that you were improving. Hope and trust that you may continue to improve. Had a letter from your mother last week. Poor soul has worried about you a lot, but she is feeling better now since she knows that you are better. I think her heart is set in that baby for it is Billy, Billy all through. You can rest contented that the children are all right. Poor Rude is the worse, poor fellow, he knows the want of you, but you will be all right after a while. When you go home you will likely go to your mama's for a while, and look out dear and don't have any more babies for two years anyway.

I suppose your husband stays with his mother while you are away.

Well, we have had a terrible rough winter and such cold weather too. This is the 18th of March and we have a roaring fire in the sitting room and another in the big kitchen stove, and looking out from where I am writing the snow is flying in torrents over the fields. I never remember of seeing such a winter. I was away last week on a sick call and am expecting another call at any moment, but it isn't far away and another in April three houses above me, so you see this is a thriving country.

Margaret told me that she wrote you a long letter. I told her over the phone that you were in the hospital so she wrote to you right away.

Jane, who was seventy-seven years old by this time, was still working as a nurse "without formal training," as she indicates.

She lived just short of three months after this letter was written.

Now my dear, I don't want you to write and fatigue yourself, don't answer this until you go home which I trust will be soon for no news is good news. So don't worrie about writing. I will likely hear from your mother before long and will hear from you through her. So don't fret or worrie about anything, but just get well as fast as you can and eat all you can.

Give my love to your dear husband and tell him that I am praying for you all. Goodbye dear. From your loving grandma, Jane Dunnet

It was unusual for Jane to end a letter by saying "goodbye." One wonders if she had a premonition that this would be the last one. She continued to give Jessie advice as she had in most of her letters. It seems to have been a close and loving relationship even though they had not seen each other since Jessie was a young girl. The letters that connected them seem to have been important to both of them.

Jessie saved letters from two family members in the previous generation, her mother and Aunt Margaret. She saved just one postcard from her mother, Anna Rose Dunnet Whitney, and it was written when Jessie was at the Portland Open Air Sanatorium in treatment for tuberculosis. Since Jessie lived in the same town as her mother, it is not surprising that there were very few letters. At the time this postcard was written, Anna Rose, Jessie's mother, was caring for Billy, who was seven months old.

Billie is fine now. He slept all night last night and is good in day time. I will write again tomorrow. Mum

One can only imagine how difficult it must have been for Jessie, in 1918, to leave her two very small children and go to the sanitarium. However, with the recent death of her sister from the same disease, she would have known that drastic measures were necessary. The letters that remain from that time were dated February and March, so she was there at least two months.

The postcard appears to be signed "Mum" though Jessie's grandchildren can only remember her referring to her mother as "Mama."

Anna Rose was married to William Hiram Whitney, and they had come to Skagit County, Washington, in 1891. William served as a county official for sixteen years, and spent more years as a city official.

Anna Rose and William Whitney

Anna Rose and William with June and Bill Pulver
in about 1920.

Anna Rose Whitney's sister, Margaret Jane Dunnet, was a schoolteacher who never married. Margaret traveled frequently and lived in different locations, though none too far from her original home.

With the exception of one postcard, which appears to have been written when Jessie was quite young, the letters from Aunt Margaret did not appear until Jessie was hospitalized, in Portland, at the Open Air Sanatorium.

Margaret Dunnet did, however, write to Jessie's older sister, Irene, when they were children. In one letter to Irene, in 1906, Margaret wrote about driving out with a horse and buggy.

There has been so little snow all winter that I have been able to drive myself almost any time I wished. Two weeks ago, to-morrow, I drove up home on the ice, intending to stay until Sunday evening, but a heavy storm came on, and I had to wait until Monday morning. Your Uncle Ed had to come back with me for a distance of three or four miles. The roads had drifted badly during the storm. I am becoming quite a driver this winter. The horse I drive is a dear little black one and so gentle. She always looks for some lump sugar before I start off with her.

Margaret was forty years old at this time, and Irene was sixteen. Margaret also told Irene about her cousins in this letter. She said she had been "up home," which is how they referred to the family home. One assumes it was the house where Jane and Edward Williston Dunnet had lived and raised their family and where Jane still lived with her son, Edward, and his family. Jane told Irene about playing with the baby, who would have been Ernest Dunnet, who was one year old.

He is very fond of his Uncle Bob (Jane's other son, Robert Forsyth Dunnet). *I believe he would leave his papa and go to him. Omar, Kathleen and Eddie sang for me.* (These are Edward Dunnet's other children, who lived with their grandmother, Jane.) *Grandma* (Jane Dunnet) *says Eddie has only one freckle*

and that covers his whole face. He doesn't like you to say any-
thing about his freckles, but he is proud of his red hair, because
it is like his papa's. (Edward was six years old at the time this
was written.)

Pictured are Margaret Dunnet and a friend.

Newcastle, Feb. 25ᵗʰ, 1918

Dear Jessie, Your grandma sent me your letter a few days ago, and I want to write to you at once to tell you how sorry I feel for you, and send you my best wishes for a speedy recovery. I feel sure you are going to get well. Be sure to keep your mind on that one thought that you are going to get well. This sounds like Christian Science, does it not?

Science, does it not? But it is not meant for that. One's mind has so much to do with the health, I think. In fact, I have proved it. I wish I were near enough to help your mother with dear little Billy. I just adore babies, in which I differ from the majority of old maids. I am not nearly as much of an old maid as I was when I visited Burlington. Ever so many sharp corners

But it is not meant for that. One's mind has so much to do with the health, I think. In fact, I have proved it. I wish I were near enough to help your mother with dear little Billy. I just adore babies, in which I differ from the majority of old maids. I am not nearly as much of an old maid as I was when I visited Burlington

What was the connotation of "old maid" in the early years of the twentieth century? Did it differ from "spinster"? Spinster was the official term for a woman who had never been married, as stated on the marriage certificates of the day. Margaret implies that the term "old maid" might have had a negative stereotype associated with it.

This is the house where Jessie and Rude lived when Billy was born. It is located on the Pulver Road in Burlington, named after Rude's parents, Anna Ammeter Pulver and Rudolph Pulver.

*have been rubbed off since then. I am
sure you girls cannot have very
pleasant recollections of your old maid
aunt. I just wish I were near enough
to show you how much I have improved
ahem! Self praise etc.. - -
I wish you and your two babies could
come east with your mother next summer.
You would certainly get well if once the
breeze from the old Miramichi filled
your lungs. It is away ahead of the
Skagit. Ask your mother if that is not true.*

*Ever so many sharp corners have been rubbed off since then. I am
sure you girls cannot have very pleasant recollections of your old
maid aunt. I just wish I were near enough to show you how much
I have improved ahem! Self praise etc.....*

I wish you and your two babies could come east with your mother next summer. You would certainly get well if once the breeze from the old Miramichi filled your lungs. <u>It is way ahead of the Skagit</u>. Ask your mother if that is not true.

It is interesting to contemplate how Margaret may have changed to become less an "old maid" type, or how she perceived that difference.

Her pride in the Miramichi River shows up in subsequent letters as well as this one. She compared the Skagit River quite unfavorably to the Miramichi even though the Skagit was quite near her sister's Burlington home.

I suppose your grandma has written to you about her French soldier. About two years ago, I put her name inside of two pairs of socks going overseas. A few days ago, she got a letter from a French soldier telling her that he had received a pair of socks with her address inside. He wrote one letter in French, and a copy in a poor translation into English. The latter said that he had received a "stocking pair."

who is a pretty fair French scholar, so he translated the letter to me. He was so much interested in the soldier that he gave me money to buy yarn for your grandma to knit him another pair. He is also answering the letter in French for mother. She is very much pleased. I suppose the spring has arrived in Portland. We have had one of the worst winters on record.

World War I, or the Great War as it was called until World War II, was continuing at this point, and everyday lives in Canada were affected by it. It is interesting that a French soldier received the socks knitted by a Canadian.

In December and January, the temperature ranged way below zero nearly every day. Many times it was 25 degrees and 30 degrees below. To-day is lovely, about 40 degrees, and the streets were quite sloppy from the melting snow.

My eyes have been giving me some trouble this winter from ill-fitting glasses, I think, so at Christmas time I decided to go to Montreal to get them treated.

Today, the trip from Miramichi to Montreal takes about nine hours on the Trans-Canada Highway. It seems it would have been a very long train trip, in 1918, to replace "ill-fitting glasses."

I made my appointment with the oculist for Dec. 27th and engaged my sleeper, but took a bad cold and had to cancel both. I am planning now to go at Easter.

This is awful scribbling, but I do not dare to use my eyes too much at one time. Now don't worry a bit and do your best to get well. With love and best wishes, I remain

Your affectionate Aunt Margaret

P.S. If you feel well enough, you might drop me a card.

This next letter was written by G. E. Crossley, who appears to be George Crossley. He appears in the 1910 Burlington census with a wife, Maude, and a six-year-old daughter, Helene, and in the 1920 census. It seems odd that he wrote instead of his wife, but that appears to be the case.

March 1st/18

Burlington, Wash.

My dear Jessie,

This is the 3rd time I have began a letter to you. My finger bothers me so that I can hardly write so please excuse everything.

We are all so glad you are getting along so nicely, & gaining so much. You will soon be home & then you will have a surprise if little Billy keeps as fat as he is. He is looking fine. Great changes around now.

This letter is difficult to transcribe as names and some words are impossible to decipher.

Walstons are going to hear Landau & Nouvaus are going with their -"Great House." Going to move into Walstons house & I hear Blanche Stevens ... house again. They moved to...

I see your folks about every second day; it has been nasty & cold until to-day - & for a ... the first of March is a beautiful day. The frost has killed all the violets so I couldn't send you any flowers, I am sending you some pictures of them.

Herb Smith is going to buy a cow, I hear. Every thing is very quiet around here & no news & I expect Rosamond tells you everything.

I did hear to-day that Bradshaw had sold out – but do not know if it is true. Their little girl has Diabetes & they ... to go to a different climate.

I am afraid you can hardly read this. My finger cramps so much. Old Mrs. Thomas has come back. They say she looks quite old or very sick; Louis Friuords is home for his examination for the army. I did not hear yet, if he has passed. All units with... love & best wishes you & hope you will soon be home.

Ever the same, G.E. Crossley

It appears that the Crossleys were friends of Jessie's parents, the Whitneys. George brought Jessie up to date on local comings and goings, and she was probably missing her home and wanting to hear local news.

On June 13, 1918, the following short article appeared in the *Bellingham Herald* in a column about happenings in Burlington. Jessie came home from the Portland Sanatorium during early June of 1918.

Will drop you a letter soon.

Denver, Colo.

July 9th

Well Jess, here I am in the large city of Denver. It really is the prettiest city I have ever seen. We have to lay over here sixteen hours. Will reach my destination some-time. W.L. Bill

This postcard came from Jessie's brother Bill and was addressed simply to Mrs. R.H. Pulver, Burlington, Wash. Bill would have been in the military at this time and, since it was wartime, he did not mention his destination.

Newcastle, Oct. 25th 1918

Dear Jessie, You will soon think that I have forgotten to answer your interesting letter received quite a while ago. I am getting dreadfully lazy about writing, I must confess. I have no excuse these days, for school has been closed since Oct. 9th on account of Spanish Influenza. We have quite a number of cases, and several have ended fatally. One sad case was a mother who died, and left eight children, the youngest about three weeks old. One of our teachers died since school closed.

Spanish flu affected every part of the world in 1918 and was devastating to young adults. It is hard to imagine the plight of the father of those eight children who had suddenly lost their mother.

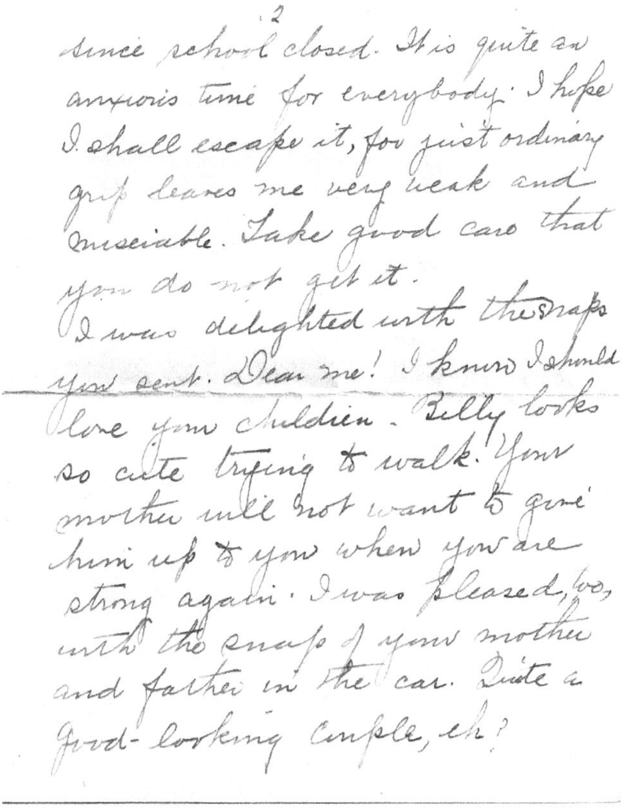

[Handwritten letter reproduced in print below]

It is quite an anxious time for everybody. I hope I shall escape it as just ordinary grip leaves me very weak and miserable. Take good care that you do not get it.

I was delighted with the snaps you sent. Dear me! I know I should love your children. Billy looks so cute trying to walk. Your mother will not want to give him up to you when you are strong again. I was pleased, too, with the snap of your mother and father in the car. Quite a good-looking couple, eh?

Jessie's first letters in the sanatorium were dated February 1918 so, by October, when this letter was written, it seems her mother was still caring for her children. How difficult that must have been for a young mother.

What have you heard from Bill lately? Has he sailed? By the report in the papers now, the end of the war is in sight. I do hope so. It has been a weary war for us, but after all, what have been our sufferings compared with France and Belgium. We scarcely realize that there is a war.

I hope you are still continuing to improve in health. Your climate is more favorable than ours, as you do not have extremes. I noticed in to-days papers that Vancouver has the influenza. Has it reached Washington yet? It seems to be all over the world just now.

When she refers to Bill here, it is Bill Whitney, Jessie's brother.

My health is very good this fall. I think I weigh more than I have for many years. I may be a fat old lady some day. Then I will send you a photo to show you my double chin.

I spent Thanksgiving Day (Oct. 14th) up home. It was a perfect day for the time of year. As it is so hard to get a doctor in the country, I am spending the holidays down here. I want to be near a doctor if I get sick.

Kind regards to all the family. Yours lovingly, Aunt Margaret

Because of her decision to stay in town over the Christmas holidays, it is obvious Margaret is still concerned about the Spanish flu epidemic. It must have been terrifying to see all the deaths their small town experienced at that time.

There are no more letters from Margaret until 1934. Whether there was a long gap in their correspondence, or the letters were lost or not saved, it is hard to say.

Chapter 3

There are just a few letters from the 1920's that survived in this collection. Jessie's son, Billie, was seven years old when he wrote the first four letters. He apparently spent a few weeks, during June 1924, with his Aunt Etta and Uncle Jess Burford. Etta was Jessie's older sister, and she and her husband lived in Raymond, Washington, which is over three hours away on today's highways and freeways. Raymond is southwest of Burlington, near the Pacific Ocean. The first letter was actually written to Billie's father, Rudolph.

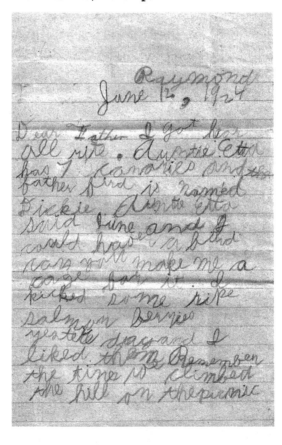

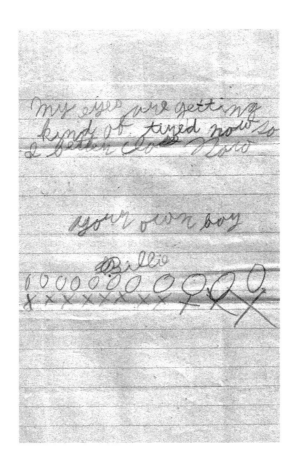

Raymond

June 12, 1924

Dear Father, I got hear all rite. Auntie Etta has 7 canaries and the father bird is named Dickie. Auntie Etta said June and I could have a bird. Can you make me a cage for it. I picked some salmon berries yesterday and I liked them. Remember the time we climbed the hill on the picnic? My eyes are getting kind of tired now so I better close now.

Your own boy,
Billie
OOOOOOOOOOXXXXXXXXX

At this point, Billie had not refined his cursive writing, but today students are usually eight years old, rather than seven, when they are taught cursive. One wonders if Etta consulted the parents before offering a bird to the child.

Five days later, Billie wrote to Jessie from Raymond.

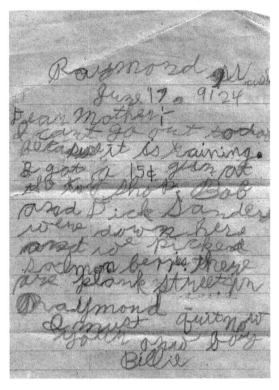

Raymond, Wash.

June 17, 9124

Dear Mother,

I can't go out today because it is raining. I got a 15 cent gun at the toy shop. Bob and Dick Sanders were down here and we picked salmon berries. There are plank streets in Raymond. I must quit now.

Your own boy,
Billie

Billie transposed the numbers in the date, but his spelling is good. The business section of Raymond had been built on stilts about six feet above the tidelands, in the early years, and the sidewalks were, in fact, planks.

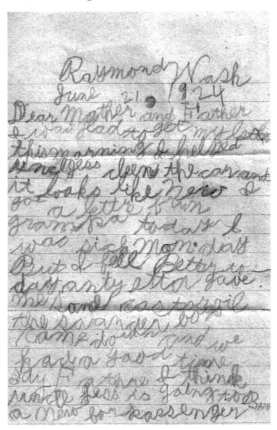

Raymond, Wash

June 21, 1924

Dear Mother and Father,

I was glad to get my letter. This morning I helped Uncle Jess cleen the car and it looks like new. I got a letter from grandpa today. I was sick Monday but I feel better today. Anty Etta gave me some castor oil. The Swander boys came down and we had a good time. Say Father, I think Uncle Jess is going to buy a new four passenger coupe. I better close because it is getting awful late now.

Your own boy, Billie

OoooooooooO XxxxxxxxxX

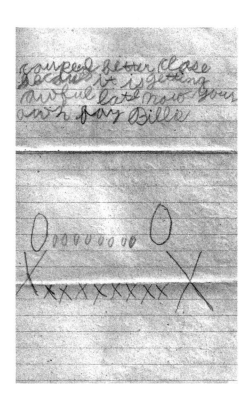

Jess Burford was a car salesman, so that may explain the interest in cars shown in this letter. Billie continued to call his parents the formal "Mother" and "Father" in his letters, and he signs them with the endearing "Your own boy, Billie."

This next letter was not written to Jessie, but to Santa Claus, so she received it and most likely treasured it.

Billie and June about the time these letters were written.

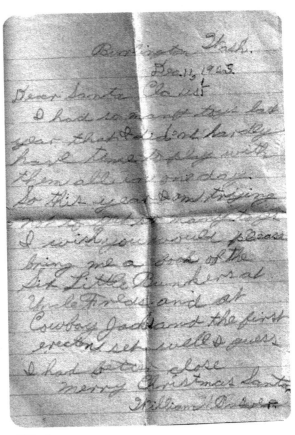

Burlington, Wash.

Dec. 11, 1925

Dear Santa Claus:

I had so many toys last year that I didn't hardly have time to play with them all in one day. So this year I am trying not to get so many toys. I wish you would please bring me a book of the Six Little Bunkers at Uncle Fred's and at Cowboy Jack and the first erector set. Well, I guess I had better close.

Merry Christmas, Santa.

William Pulver

In the year and a half since the last letter, Bill's handwriting had certainly improved. Also, he was a little more formal in this letter to Santa than the ones to his parents.

The first erector set was called "Mysto Erector Structural Steel Builder" and was first sold in 1913. It quickly became a very popular toy for children and remained so for more than fifty years.

The next postcard was addressed to Jessie, Rudolph, Etta, and Jess and was sent by Billie when he was in school. It was mailed to the Chevrolet Garage in Raymond where Jess worked. Jessie and Rudolph must have been visiting the Burfords at that time.

Dear Aunty Etta and Uncle Jess mother and Daddy I am writing at school self guess had better hurry I guess I will give you a lot of kisses and hugs. XXXX OOOO your own boy Billie.

Dear Aunty Etta and Uncle Jess Mother and Daddy

I am writing at school so I guess I had better hurry. I guess I will give you a lot of kisses and hugs.

XXXXOOOO

Your own boy, Billie

Burlington, Wash.

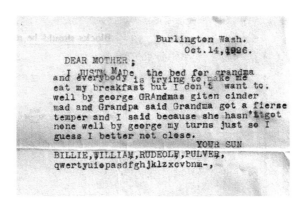

Oct. 14, 1926

Dear Mother;

I just made the bed for grandma and everybody is trying to make me eat my breakfast but I don't want to. Well by George Grandma's gitten kinder mad and Grandpa said Grandma got a fierse temper and I said because she hasn't got none. Well by George my turns just so I guess I better not close.

Your sun

Billie, William, Rudeolf, Pulver

Qwertyieopasdfghjklzcbbnm-,

Billie had somehow gotten his hands on a typewriter, and it seems he was just being a silly nine-year-old boy in this letter. Jessie probably saved it because she was amused by it.

This valentine was made by June for Jessie, Rude, and Billie.
June addressed her parents formally, as Billie did. Her neat and
careful handwriting showed concentration and care.

Chapter 4

Letters to Jessie from her aunt, Margaret Jane Dunnet, resumed in 1934. There may have been letters in the interim but, if so, they did not survive to become part of this collection. Margaret was sixty-eight years old in 1934. Jessie was thirty-eight, and her children, June and Bill, were seventeen and eighteen. Jessie worked with Rudolph on the family farm, where they had milk cows and raised strawberries, sugar beets, hay, and other crops on forty acres.

Though no letters to Jessie remain that were written before 1934, there are several from 1932 to Jessie's daughter June when she was sixteen. Margaret wrote, in September, during a trip to Maine to visit distant relatives.

"For the first time in all my journeys to the USA I had to pay a head tax of eight dollars. Of course, I will get it back when I return home, but it inconvenienced me somewhat. I suppose the coming election makes the officers particular. For the first time in eighteen years Maine went Democrat, and the saying has always been 'as Maine goes, so goes the Union.'"

Margaret's reference to Maine going Democrat refers not to the presidential election of 1932, but the state election for governor and congress held two months earlier. On November 8th of that year, Maine voted for Herbert Hoover for president, at 55.83 percent, so they actually voted Republican then.

The letters from June's Great-aunt Margaret must have been quite important to her as she retyped them and saved them in a notebook, and that notebook of letters is still intact today.

On October 9th, 1933, Margaret wrote to June.

I was pleased, indeed, to get your letter not long ago. How nice for you to be going to business college and staying with your grand-

dad, and how nice for him to have you for company! It seems to be such a good arrangement – a mutual benefit. Of course, you will miss the home folks, and I know how much they will miss you, but you are not far away from them. I would love to see you all again, but suppose that will never be.

In January of 1934, Margaret wrote another letter to June.

The weather is so cold to-night that my thoughts may congeal before they reach the point of my pen. This morning the mercury registered 30 below zero. I have a smelly oil stove in my room tonight to keep my fingers from getting stiff. This is a very cold house. My landlady sits most of the time in the kitchen, so she does not know how cold it is upstairs. But spring will soon be here, I hope. You have probably green fields by this time. Would love to fly there for a while. We have not had a winter like this in memory of the oldest inhabitants.

The average January temperature in Miramichi over the past twenty-five years has been 12.6 degrees Fahrenheit, considerably warmer than the thirty below zero that Margaret spoke of in 1934.

By April 5th of that year, there was still snow on the ground in Miramichi, and Margaret wrote to June about it.

It is almost a month since I have received your letter (three weeks, at least). I have not been feeling quite as well as usual. Spring laziness, I think. When we lose the snow, and the grass begins to look green, I shall probably feel better. We still have heaps of snow on the sides of the street where it was ploughed during the winter. The bus, between here and Chatham cannot get on the road yet. Of course, this has been an unusual winter. Don't let these reports prevent you from coming east some day. Our summers are ideal. Your grandpa will tell you about them. And you will love the river. There is only <u>one</u> Miramichi River in the world (the literal truth).

Later in the summer of 1934, Jessie received this letter from Margaret:

Whitneyville, June 27th, 1934

Dear Jessie,

It is about time that I answered your very interesting letter which I received quite a long time ago. I am getting dreadfully slow about writing letters. Old age or laziness (perhaps both) are the cause. I gave up my room in town on May 17th, and for a while visited around in Chatham and in Newcastle. I am settling down now at the old home for a while. Your Aunt May and I have been making dresses for her grandchildren to wear to the closing exercises of their school.

Last Friday night, I attended the Graduating exercises of Harkins Academy in Newcastle. About 40, actually 42, graduated. The exercises were very interesting, consisting of songs, class prophecy, valedictory, presentation of prizes and addresses. Some distant relatives of yours and mine were in the class. The mothers of three of the girls are my second cousins. Far away, of course, but the fact added interest. Besides, several were former pupils of mine. The invited guests filled the auditorium, so others had to stand.

I must write to Etta for her birthday July 7th, although she owes me a letter.

All these years after their grandmother, Jane Dunnet, had complained about Etta not writing regularly, it was a source of frustration for Margaret.

I do not hear from Rosamond at all. I always send a card at Christmas. I owe your father a letter, and will write soon. My debt to you is of longer standing.

You asked me the date of Mother's death. It was June 11th, 1918. Anything you would like to know, just make a list of questions, and I will try to get the information.

I am receiving papers and some letters from Scotland, in which I am getting some news of my relatives there. I think your grandmother Whitney came from the same part of Scotland as your great-grandfather Dunnet did - Caithness - up in the north.

By this time, Jessie's mother had died, having lived to only sixty-one years of age. Margaret continued to correspond with her brother-in-law, however, as she mentioned in several letters to Jessie. Margaret touched on the date her mother, Jane, had died. This was a difficult time for Anna Rose to lose her mother. It was shortly after the death of her daughter Irene, Jessie was ill with tuberculosis, and Anna Rose was still caring for the baby, Billy.

Margaret carried on a lifetime correspondence with the Dunnet family in Scotland. Her grandparents had emigrated from Scotland, in 1823, with an infant daughter, Catherine. Interestingly, they left behind their two-year-old son, with his paternal grandfather. This son, William, never left Scotland, and he married and raised a family there. His descendants are the family with whom Margaret corresponded.

Caithness is the home of the Sinclairs. Perhaps your father knows. In the papers which I receive from Caithness, the name of Sinclair occurs very often.

I have a new dress – navy silk with white dot, and a plain navy silk coat. It is quite becoming. Wish I were young enough to wear a white hat with it.

When I read over the familiar names in the Burlington paper you sent me, I felt so very lonely, and sad. The names brought back memories of the happy days I spent there with your dear mother and with all the family.

Margaret described her new outfit here, but bemoaned the fact that she was too old to wear a white hat. Was that the custom of the time, or was it a personal decision?

Jessie's paternal grandmother, William Hiram Whitney's mother, was Jessie Sinclair. Jessie Whitney Pulver was named after her as well as William Hiram's sister, Jessie Whitney. Jessie's middle name, Alberta, was after her mother's sister, Alberta May Dunnet.

Jessie was interested in her family history, so Margaret sent her the following information about the Forsyth and Dunnet family tree. Jessie's grandmother, Jane Dunnet, was a Forsyth.

Forsyth 3

Robert Forsyth. Senior married Jane Marten, daughter of William and Mary Ann Martin Their son Robert married Margaret McKinnon. Her father fought with the British in the Revolutionary War. Robert Forsyth. Senior was an officer with the British army in the Revolutionary War He and Gregor McKinnon were Loyalists, so they received grants of land from Britain in 1783. They landed in Saint John. N.B on May 18th 1783. Robert Forsyth Jr. and Margaret McKinnon had seven children among them Jane, (my mother). Ann was another daughter (She was "Auntie Rogers" to your family

Forsyth

Robert Forsyth Senior married Jane Martin, daughter of William and Mary Ann Martin. Their son Robert married Margaret McKinnon. Her father fought with the British in the Revolutionary War. Robert Forsyth Senior was an officer with the British Army in the Revolutionary War. He and Gregor McKinnon were Loyalists, so they received grants of land from Britain in 1783. They landed in Saint John, New Brunswick on May 18th, 1783.

Robert Forsyth Jr. and Margaret McKinnon had seven children, among them Jane, (my mother). Ann was another daughter (She was "Auntie Rogers" to your family).

Auntie Rogers, or Ann Forsyth, is the Aunt Ann that Jane

Dunnet referred to in some of her letters. Annie Rogers lived in Oscoda, Michigan for a time. She was married to Anthony Rogers, and they had two children. Jessie had a book inscribed with Annie's name. Annie Rogers shows up in the 1900 Burlington census as a resident. She was seventy-two years old at the time, and she had immigrated to the United States, in 1860, at age twenty-two. Annie was shown as owning her own home, and she was a widow.

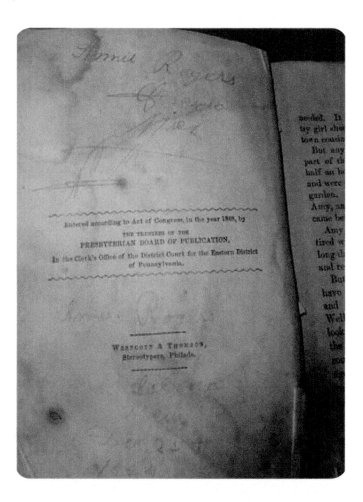

This note, in Jessie's distinctive handwriting, was in a book which is now in the possession of Cameron Kunz, Jessie's great-great-granddaughter.

John Dunnet of Scotland married Ann Nicholson. They came to British North America (Canada) bringing their daughter Catherine in 1823. They left their eldest son with his grandfather. This son William did not come afterwards to Canada. The Dunnets of Caithness Scotland are his descendants.

John's son Edward married Jane Forsyth. They had ten children. Your mother, "Annie Rose" was the sixth child. I was the fourth.

This is all I can tell you of the Dunnets.

Can you build a family tree from this information? Your mother was named "Annie Rose", registered in the Family Bible. not "Anna". She always signed her name "Rose" in all my letters. At school she usually got "Annie Rose", as there was another Annie Dunnet. The "Annie" was for mother's sister; the "Rose" for her friend. Etta told me that your mother always signed her name "Anna." but never in my memory. Your father always called her "Rose" when I visited them.
We are on the watch for Bill Forsyth. Wish Charlotte could have come. We are having hot weather now. Love -
     Aunt Margaret.

Can you build a family tree from this information? Your mother was named "Annie Rose", registered in the Family Bible. Not "Anna". She always signed her name "Rose" in all my letters. At school she usually got "Annie Rose" as there was another Annie Dunnet. The "Annie" was for mother's sister, the "Rose" for her friend. Etta told me that your mother always signed her name "Anna", but <u>never</u> in my memory. Your father always called her "Rose" when I visited them.

We are on watch for Bill Forsyth. Wish Charlotte could have come.

We are having hot weather now. Love, Aunt Margaret

Margaret seemed quite adamant about her sister's name here. Because there is only one postcard from Anna Rose, we learn little about her from these letters. Why did she change her name from Annie to Anna? Her headstone says Anna Rose. It is in the Whitney section of the Burlington Cemetery near a large headstone that simply says Whitney. Her daughter, Irene Whitney Dawson, is buried near Anna Rose in the Whitney section.

Newcastle, Jan'y 7th, 1935

Dear Jessie –

Congratulations! Have you moved into your new home yet? Yes, I think I remember where the fair grounds are. If only you could avoid paying duty, I would send you something for your new home, but the duty takes all the pleasure away. I shall be glad to get a snap of your new home with the people who live in it.

I have not heard from your father since early in October...

This is the house Rudolph and Jessie moved into in 1934. By this time, the work horses had been replaced by an Allis-Chalmers tractor that Rude had purchased from his brother, Fred. Their grandchildren's earliest memories were of visiting this house.

Was sorry to hear that he had not been well. Perhaps it is a blessing in disguise that he did not win in his election. He can have a life free from worry now. A good rest is surely coming to him for he had been an efficient and faithful worker.

I am going to suggest to him when I write, that he takes one of the "cent-a-mile" trips east to see all his old friends. The tickets, last year, were good for forty-five days. That would probably be as long as we could hold him.

There is nothing to indicate that William did, in fact, take that trip to New Brunswick.

The change would do him a world of good. And wouldn't we try to give him a good time!! I suspect that if he went to your Aunt Marjorie's for a visit, he would not spare much for the rest, as she is quite like your mother in many ways. I sent him a pair of all wool hand-knit socks. They were too late for Christmas, but I hope he got them at the New Year. I sent them "over the line" by a friend who was going home for his Christmas holidays. He said he would mail them as soon as he got there.

Margaret was concerned about the duty that people had to pay, at that time, on packages sent from Canada to the US. When she said she sent them "over the line," she meant that she had sent them to Maine, so they could be mailed from there, thus avoiding the duty fee.

Aunt Marjorie, referred to here, was Anna Rose and Margaret's younger sister. She lived near Margaret, was married, and had five children. Her eldest daughter was named Annie Rose after her sister, Anna Rose Dunnet Whitney.

Your father would have no duty to pay on them.

Santa Claus was very kind to me this year. Among my gifts were two boxes of handkerchiefs, two boxes of chocolates, a bottle of black currant preserves, a bottle of honey, two pairs of silk stockings and a pair of woolen ones, three boxes of stationery, a hand-painted picture (framed) a calendar, a bottle of talcum powder, two packs *of cards (boxed) and I know so little about cards, a basket of fruit and candy, a chicken, a pound of butter, a perfume bottle and a bottle of perfume, $10, and some lovely cards - about fifty. Everybody was very kind to me...*

Margaret must have been in close contact with many people to receive so many Christmas gifts. She mentions all her gifts for birthdays and Christmases in subsequent letters as well.

> *I forgot to mention a lovely linen tea-cloth from a cousin I have
> never seen in Scotland. On each corner is the "willow pattern" in
> dark blue. You know, the pattern is the same as on dishes. Your
> great-grandmother had some of the "willow pattern" dishes. They
> are worth a lot of money now. I also forgot a pretty brooch and a
> small change purse. Everything is very useful.*

I forgot to mention a lovely linen tea-cloth from a cousin I have never seen in Scotland. On each corner is the "willow pattern" in dark blue. You know, the pattern is the same as on dishes. Your great-grandmother had some of the "willow pattern" dishes. They are worth a lot of money now. I also forgot a pretty brooch and a small change purse. Everything is very useful.

Have you a radio? We heard England, Scotland, Ireland, Australia,

New Zealand, India and South Africa on Christmas day. The program lasted an hour, and then King George spoke to all parts of the Empire. We heard his speech distinctly.

The first radio address by an English monarch to the British Empire had been just two years earlier, in 1932, when King George V addressed the Empire. It was George V, again, giving the address that Margaret described here.

Jessie and Rude did, in fact, have a radio. This information was recorded in the 1930 census in the US.

And of course, we heard the royal wedding several weeks ago. It was very distinct. The "I do" was as plain as if they were in the room.

I would love to catch a glimpse of your father's garden. How did Rosamond look? I never hear from her. Does she still live in Ray-

mond? That is where I addressed her card. Received a card from Bill and Faye with a little note written inside. Was very glad to hear from them. I also received a card from Anna Nichols. She told me that she had not been very well, but was still teaching. Please excuse this scrappy letter. Will write to June soon. Love to all.

Lovingly, Aunt Margaret

This is a photo of the royal wedding that Margaret referred to. It was the first royal wedding to ever be broadcast on radio, and was the marriage of Prince Albert and Elizabeth Bowes-Lyon. He would later become King George VI. Margaret was very interested in the royal family, followed their lives, and referred to them often in her letters.

Newcastle, May 16th, 1935

Dear Jessie –

I am not a very prompt correspondent, as I noticed April 6th on your letter. The days slip away so quickly since spring has come.

I was pleased to get the picture of your house. How I wish I could see the inside of it! June described it so well that I could almost see it. You spoke about making doughnuts with sour cream and asking if my recipe was the same. I made some last week, and they were pretty good. Your Uncles Ed and Bob usually bring me cream every week.

Last week it got sour, so I made the doughnuts. I use one cup sour cream, 1 cup of sugar, 2 eggs, salt, nutmeg, and 1 teaspoon of soda sifted in the flour. When I cut them out, I leave them on the board to rise about an hour. Then when I put them in the fat to cook, I turn them over on the board because the top, having risen, it is a little rough. Have I made myself understood? But I know yours are far better than mine. I like the kind of flour that you people have in the west for cakes.

I thought I had more paper in my tablet, but when I took this out, behold it was empty. I must search for some more. I am dreadfully extravagant with note paper.

I am planning to break up housekeeping in a few weeks' time. Have been invited to Moncton, a city of about 20,000, not far from Newcastle, perhaps 80 miles. I cannot get any new clothes for the visit. My friends will have to take me for myself, not my clothes. My tweed suit is still in style, my dress of last summer looks quite respectable, and my knitted suit can be worn with comfort for quite a long time, as our warm weather does not come until the middle of June.

Your Uncle Ed's second son, Edward, (too) had a very narrow escape from death last week. He was working on a lumber drive, and volunteered to go out and break a "jam". This is rather dangerous work. He went out, but the logs started, and he was taken over the falls with the logs over him. He was rescued, unconscious, but after a time he recovered. He was hurried to the hospital here and "X-rayed". There were no broken bones, but he was badly bruised. I am going down to see him again this afternoon.

This is a reminder of the dangers of logging then and now. There was also danger in the fishing industry, which was a big part of the economy of this region.

This is his third accident. One spring, he had his leg broken in three places.

Did you have a visit from Bill? You said that you expected him sometime in April. I received a long interesting letter from Anna Nichols about Christmas time. Did I tell you about it before? She paid such a lovely tribute to your mother and father. I fancy that a happy married life appealed to her. Hers has not been a success.

I enjoyed June's last letter ever so much. I must write to her soon. Love to Etta and her family when you see her. Irene must be quite a big girl now. With love to the Pulver Quartette, I remain yours lovingly, Aunt Margaret

I have not heard from your father for a long time. I do enjoy his letters. Address Newcastle, as usual.

The Irene referred to here was the daughter of Etta Burford and was Jessie's niece. Irene was actually born to Rosamond, but when Rosamond and her husband divorced, Irene went to live with Etta, and Rosamond raised Irene's younger sister, Marjorie. Irene was named for Rosamond and Jessie's sister who died of tuberculosis as a young adult. Marjorie may have been named after Rosamond's great-aunt, Margaret's sister. There was a tradition of naming children after family members, so it is possible.

It's hard to know if the Bill referred to in this letter is Jessie's brother Bill or her nephew Bill. Either of them could have come to visit William Hiram and other family members. There were many Williams in this family, including Jessie's son, Bill.

These were the Williams in Jessie's life at this time. From left, they are William E. Whitney (her nephew), William Whitney Pulver (her son), William E. Whitney (her brother), and William Hiram Whitney (her father). Numerous descendants of William Pulver carry his name as their middle name.

Newcastle, Jan'y 6th, 1936

Dear Jessie –

As I went away to Fredericton (our capital city) to spend the holiday season, I am late in acknowledging my Christmas remembrances. Many thanks for the pretty handkerchief. It is one of my favorite gifts. I did very little for my friends this year. Did not feel well for several weeks before Christmas. I managed to knit a pair of socks for your Dad, but had to wait to give them to a friend to mail in the USA so he probably will be late getting them.

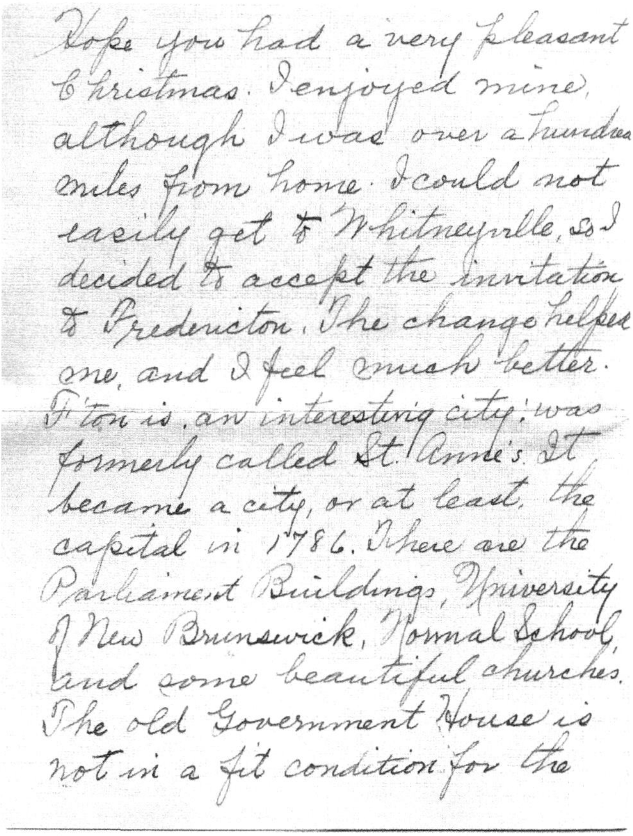
Hope you had a very pleasant
Christmas. I enjoyed mine,
although I was over a hundred
miles from home. I could not
easily get to Whitneyville, so I
decided to accept the invitation
to Fredericton. The change helped
me, and I feel much better.
F'ton is an interesting city; was
formerly called St. Anne's. It
became a city, or at least, the
capital in 1786. There are the
Parliament Buildings, University
of New Brunswick, Normal School,
and some beautiful churches.
The old Government House is
not in a fit condition for the

Hope you had a very pleasant Christmas. I enjoyed mine although I was over a hundred miles from home. I could not easily get to Whitneyville, so I decided to accept the invitation to Fredericton. The change helped me, and I feel much better. F'ton is an interesting city; was formerly called St. Anne's. It became a city or at least the capital in 1786. There are the Parliament Buildings, University of New Brunswick, Normal School, and some beautiful churches. The old Government House is not in a fit condition for the Lieut. Governor to live in, so it has been made into a barracks for the Royal Northwest Mounted Police.

Lieut. Governor to live in, so it has been made into a barracks for the Royal Northwest Mounted Police.

Santa Claus was very kind to me. One of my gifts was $10, which enabled me to take the trip. Did I ever send you the names of your mother's ancestors on both sides - the Dunnets and Forsyths? It seems to me that you asked me. Anna Nichols asked me for some information. She wanted to know something about "a coat of arms". Think of a good American wanting such a thing! Well, I believe the Forsyths away back, had a

---

Santa Claus was very kind to me. One of my gifts was $10, which enabled me to take the trip. Did I ever send you the names of your mother's ancestors on both sides – the Dunnets and Forsyths? It seems to me that you asked me. Anna Nichols asked me for some information. She wanted to know something about "a coat of arms". Think of a good American wanting such a thing!

*'coat of arms', but if the Dunnets
had one it would probably
have been a broom, mop,
hoe and shovel intertwined,
because all of them had to
work hard.
Was'nt it lovely of Bill to
send me Christmas greetings
and the "hanky"? Boys, as a
rule, do not think of these things
What a comfort your children
are to you! Please tell June that
I hope to write to her when I
get back some snaps which
I sent to be finished. They
are snow scenes, and if good,*

Well, I believe the Forsyths away back had a "coat of arms", but if the Dunnets had one it would probably have been a broom, mop, hoe and shovel intertwined, because all of them had to work hard.

Wasn't it lovely of Bill to send me Christmas greetings and the hanky? Boys, as a rule, do not think of these things. What a comfort your children are to you! Please tell June that I hope to write to her when I get back some snaps which I sent to be finished. They are snow scenes, and if good will send one.

will send one

We have had a marvellous winter for our country. Yesterday, I was invited to Chatham to take dinner with my adopted family, the McDonalds, at the house of a mutual friend. I went by bus and found the roads just about as smooth as in summer. A huge snow plough keeps them in good condition. The friends brought me back to Newcastle.

Received a card from Etta. Wish she would write me some time. I wrote her a long time ago, but she did not reply, neither does Rosamond, but perhaps they are very busy.

We have had a marvelous winter for our country. Yesterday I was invited to Chatham to take dinner with my adopted family, the McDonalds, at the house of a mutual friend. I went by bus and found the roads just about as smooth as in summer. A huge snow plough keeps them in good condition. The friends brought me back to Newcastle.

Received a card from Etta. Wish she would write me some time. I wrote her a long time ago, but she did not reply. Neither does Rosamond, but perhaps they are very busy.

I enjoy June's letters ever so much. She writes me, just as if I were her age, and you don't know how much I like that. One hates to be thought too old to take an interest in young people's affairs. I took a little girl of eleven to a tea room as her Christmas treat, and wasn't she thrilled? She felt quite grown up.

I received a card from Mrs. Haviland, Vancouver. She and her husband were at your mothers' for lunch one day on their way home from New Brunswick.

also one from Mrs. Ingram who
also visited your mother. Mrs
Atkinson also sent me a card.
I think I received over fifty. One
of my gifts was a blue linen
tea-cloth from a Dunnet
cousin in the north of Scotland.
If you look at a map of Scotland
you will see Dunnet Head.
This cousin lives near that
place in the county of Caithness.
Wishing you all a happy
New Year, I remain
    Yours lovingly,
    Aunt Margaret

...also one from Mrs. Ingram who also visited your mother. Mrs. Atkinson also sent me a card. I think I received over fifty. One of my gifts was a blue linen tea-cloth from a Dunnet cousin in the north of Scotland. If you look at a map of Scotland you will see Dunnet Head. This cousin lives near that place in the county of Caithness. Wishing you all a happy new year, I remain, yours lovingly, Aunt Margaret

Newcastle, Dec. 26th, 1936

Dear Jessie –

How can I thank you all for your share in the lovely gift of flowers. They arrived on Christmas Eve from Snowballs Greenhouse in Chatham. They are huge, yellow "mums", and look even better to-day than they did when they arrived. They have been much admired by all my friends who have called since. It was certainly a lovely thought which prompted you to send them. Just now, when I am not feeling very well, they were doubly welcome. I am writing your father too, to-night.

Yesterday the folks with whom I live, invited me to dinner along with a mutual friend, and I enjoyed it ever so much.

All my friends were exceedingly kind to me this Christmas. First of all, I was invited to spend the season in Fredericton, but it is a distance of over a hundred miles, and the weather is cold, so I decided not to go. These friends sent me a hot-water bottle with a crocheted cover with my initial on it. Another friend in Moncton, sent me an all-wool blanket trimmed on edges with satin, of peach color.

Even though these letters were written in the 1930's, during the depression that affected most of the world, it was not mentioned in Margaret's letters, nor did she talk about "hard times." The only suggestion of lack of money is in some of the Christmas gifts she received, chickens, butter, and stamps.

Another friend sent a hot water bottle with cover. These three friends are doing their share keeping me warm.

The McDonalds, where I spent some time several years ago, mothering them, brought their usual remembrance - a basket of fruit and $10. My Scotch friends in Chatham brought me a basket of fruit and grape jelly. An interesting gift came from Scotland - an all-time calendar with a picture of a ship under the glass. I also received cards from other cousins in Scotland. Jean Swanson said that she had lost June's address, and could not send her a card. When I write to her, I will send it. I received two photos, two boxes of hankies, several inside of cards; box of chocolates; two pairs of stockings, a year's subscription to "Ladies Home Journal", and the same to "Canadian Home Journal", a calendar, framed motto, and a box of stationery, some butter and a chicken from home; box of cake, and a chicken from your Aunt Marjorie's family; a dozen of eggs from a cousin, plum loaf and mince patties from friends in town, eighty-eight cards and letters, June's book and hdkf (handkerchief) Her card was very good - strongly Scotch. Please tell her that I will write her very soon. Among my letters was a nice one from your father. He certainly writes an interesting letter.

Anna Nichols wrote me also.

3

My grocer gave me a pretty calendar of the "Quintuplets." They are each playing with a toy. I saw the picture "Reunion" with the quints this fall. Have you seen it yet? Last night I saw Shirley Temple in "Dimples" - very good. Last week, Jack McDonald took me to Chatham to see "Mary, Queen of Scotland". Katherine Hepburn is a wonderful actress, and the one who played Queen Elizabeth was also good.

Well British history has been making lately. Never before did a king of the Empire abdicate because of a woman - and such a woman. If she had only been a decent one, I do not mean her divorces, but the fact that she broke up two homes to get her husbands, and now the ex-king broke up the home to get her. If no other punishment befalls them, their memories will not be pleasant. We are *well rid of a king who thought so lightly of his Empire. <u>We</u> would never accept her. Had she been a single, refined American girl, no one would have objected. In fact, it would be a good alliance. Think of Queen Mary's crown resting on Wally's head!!*

A distant cousin – in fact a second cousin of yours lives in Bermuda. If you or family collects stamps, I can send you one or two.

Margaret definitely had strong opinions about British royalty. She refers here to King Edward, who succeeded his father, King George V, in January of 1936. He proposed to Wallis Simpson, an American who had been divorced and was in the process of another divorce. This was not acceptable to the British, and so after 326 days of his reign, King Edward abdicated and his brother, Albert, became King George VI.

The quintuplets Margaret referred to here were the Dionne quints, who were born in Canada and were the first known quintuplets to survive. They were taken away from their parents for their first nine years and raised by the government, which made a lot of money from endorsements and using them as a tourist attraction. Several movies were made of them, including *Reunion*, in 1936, when they were two years old.

I have received a few of the ex-king's stamps. Canada has not printed any. They can only be obtained from Britain.

The home folks are in their usual health. Kathleen has not been well lately. She was down to see the doctor to-day. Her nerves are bad. I am feeling better to-day and yesterday. Some repair work has been going on in this house and the noise has irritated my poor nerves, but it is now done. This is badly written owing to cold hands. This is a cold house. Again thanking you for the lovely flowers. I remain yours lovingly, Aunt Margaret. Happy New Year.

My Christmas card to Rosamond was returned last year, and this year I did not have her new address. Please tell her, and sometime send it to me.

Margaret showed an interest in stamps, but she did not indicate that she collected them herself, only that others might be interested in the stamps she could get.

In a letter to June at about this time, Margaret said, "When you write, be sure to tell me your boyfriend's surname. I was so pleased to get the snaps. You two are certainly the 'long and short' of it. I like his appearance."

Glen Gee and June Pulver

Whitneyville, May 20th, 1937

Dear Jessie –

I have been a long time answering your good letter. This spring, I have been very slow about everything, as I was not feeling very well. Now, that I am home again, I am feeling better already. Nerves seemed to be the principal disease, and they can cause lots of discomfort, such as indigestion and sleeplessness. I am sleeping now, day and night.

We have quite a late spring this year, even if we had a mild winter. The ice was two weeks later going out of the river. The lumber drives are nearly all in the main river, so that will be a great thing for the working men.

a great thing for the working men. Wages, on the drives, was much higher this year. I suppose farming in your county is well advanced. The winter frosts killed a lot of hay and the strawberry crop will be poor. How are your strawberries? The home folks are feeling better. Your Aunt May is still lame; the doctor said that it will take two more months to get over the spraining of the ligaments in her leg. Kathleen's arm, on the side where the operation was, is still a bit sore. To add to the troubles Ernest's wife had to go to the hospital for some treatment, but she is getting better. The other relatives are in good health. I was interested to hear about the Forsyth's visits to you. Lois

Wages, on the drives, was much higher this year. I suppose farming in your country is well advanced. The winter frosts killed a lot of hay and the strawberry crop will be poor. How are your strawberries?

The home folks are feeling better. Your Aunt May is still lame; the doctor said that it will take two more months to get over the spraining of the ligaments in her leg. Kathleen's arm, on the side where the operation was, is still a bit sore. To add to the troubles, Ernest's wife had to go to the hospital for some treatment, but she is getting better. The other relatives are in good health.

I was interested to hear about the Forsyth's visits to you.

Lumber drives were held in the spring, in logging towns, when the ice broke up on the rivers. Trees were logged and hauled to the rivers in the winter, and skilled men drove the logs downriver. It was dangerous work, but New Brunswick was a logging province, so many men earned their living this way.

3.

was a nice girl as I remember her. Do you ever see Anna Nichols? We had quite a celebration here on Coronation day. I sent one of the stamps to June. Did she get her "airmail" birthday + card? I was a little late in getting it off - May 1st, but I thought it ought to get there by the 5th. I sent Willie Dunnet's, Tacoma also by airmail. I am expecting some coronation stamps from Scotland. As soon as we get our new coins, I must send you one. We are going to have silver dollars for the first time, for common use. There was one to commemorate King George's jubilee, but they were only in a short time. The new ones will be for permanent use. I saw by to-days paper that Edward, Duke of Windson

Lois as I remember her. Do you ever see Anna Nichols?

We had quite a celebration here on Coronation Day. I sent one of the stamps to June. Did she get her "airmail" birthday card? I was a little late in getting it off - May 1st, but I thought it ought to get there by the 5th. I sent Willie Dunnet's, Tacoma also by airmail. I am expecting some coronation stamps from Scotland. As soon as we get our new coins, I must send you one. We are going to have silver dollars for the first time, for common use. There was one to commemorate King George's jubilee, but they were only in a short time. The new ones will be for permanent use. I saw by to-day's paper that Edward, Duke of Windsor is to marry his "love" on June 3rd. Good luck to them! But she will tire of him too. Hope she does. He will not have enough money to suit her, but she will get what she was looking for - a title. Of course she planned to be queen, but Stanley Baldwin and the British Cabinet "threw a monkey wrench into the machinery" and that failed. She did the British Empire a favor when she "vamped" Edward off the throne. He is quite dissipated, so I have heard. We have a good ruler now, much like his father, who was the best king we ever had. The queen is Scotch which will help.

The little girl which I "mothered" just after I was in the West went over to the coronation with her father. She will have a great time. Hope all the family and relatives are well. My best love to all.

Yours lovingly, Aunt Margaret

Stanley Baldwin, referred to here, was prime minister of Britain at this time, and he led the cabinet in rejecting Edward as King if he married Wallis Simpson. Margaret continues to speak disparagingly of both the former king and his bride.

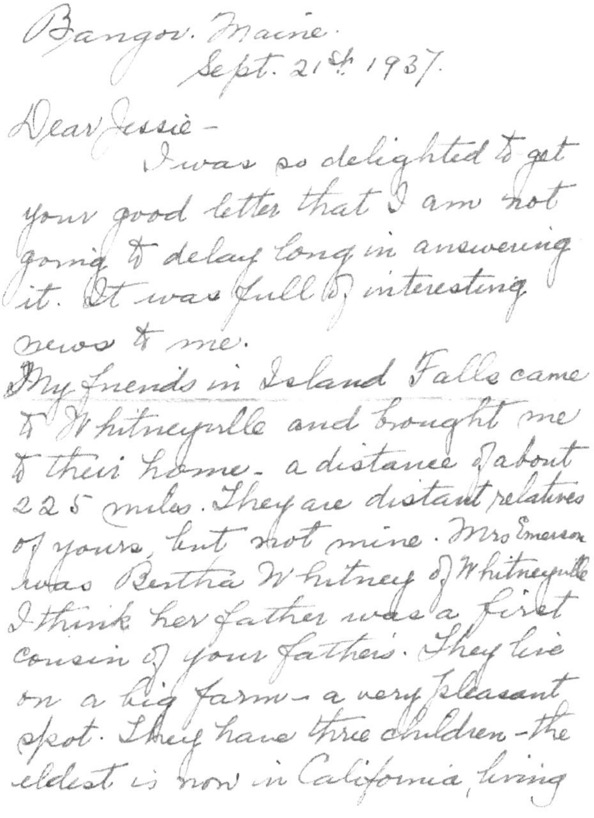

[Handwritten letter reproduction:]

Bangor, Maine.
Sept. 21st 1937.

Dear Jessie –

I was so delighted to get your good letter that I am not going to delay long in answering it. It was full of interesting news to me.

My friends in Island Falls came to Whitneyville and brought me to their home – a distance of about 225 miles. They are distant relatives of yours, but not mine. Mrs. Emerson was Bertha Whitney of Whitneyville I think her father was a first cousin of your father's. They live on a big farm – a very pleasant spot. They have three children – the eldest is now in California, living

---

Bangor, Maine September 21st, 1937

Dear Jessie,

I was so delighted to get your good letter that I am not going to delay long in answering it. It was full of interesting news to me.

My friends in Island Falls came to Whitneyville and brought me to their home - a distance of about 225 miles. They are distant relatives of yours, but not mine. Mrs. Emerson was Bertha Whitney of Whitneyville. I think her father was a first cousin of your father's. They live on a big farm - a very pleasant spot. They have three children - the eldest is now in California, living With his uncle - Arthur Whitney, Santa Ana and going to college. After I finish my visit here I return to Island Falls, then early in October, I plan to go home.

I am feeling much stronger. I think the change has helped me. I am staying here with the only Scotch relative that I have ever seen. She was Elsie Dunnet of Edinburgh. We have interesting talks of Scotland.

with his uncle – Arthur Whitney Santa Ana. and going to college after I finish my visit here, I return to Island Falls, then early in October, I plan to go home. I am feeling much stronger. I think the change has helped me. I am staying here with the only Scotch relative that I have ever seen. She was Elsie Dunnet of Edinburgh. We have interesting talks of Scotland. I was so pleased to get cards from your father and Bill in Vancouver. Bill sent me the paper which had an account of Billy's brave deed.

I was so pleased to get cards from your father and Bill in Vancouver. Bill sent me the paper which had an account of Billy's brave deed.

Does your Humane Society give medals to people for brave deeds? I think he deserves one.

I do enjoy June's letters. Yes, I imagine from her letters that Glenn is the one and only. Well, he is a lucky fellow. I was interested in what you told me of the doings of Etta, Rosamond, Bill and family, the Forsyths. It is nice that they have their own home now.

I visited the new airport in Houlton the day it was opened. I have a first cover which I prize. Now this is not worth calling a letter. Will do better when I go home. Love to all your family. Your loving Aunt Margaret

P.S. Do you ever see Anna Nichols?

Anna Nichols, who Margaret asked about here and in other letters, was the daughter of Anna Forsyth Rogers, Jane Dunnet's sister, making her Margaret's first cousin. Anna Nichols was born in Michigan, in 1875, and married John Dustin Nichols. Anna and John were orchardists in the Yakima, Washington, area from around 1910 to at least 1924. In addition to that, John was in real estate, and Anna was Superintendent of Yakima County Schools, according to newspaper reports and the 1910 census. In the early 1930's, Anna Nichols was a principal at Maury School in the King County School District. The following article addresses her tenure as superintendent. It appeared in the *Yakima Herald* in 1921.

YAKIMA SUPERINTENDENT APPOINTS COUNTY BOARD

Miss Mae Clark, who became Yakima County school superintendent in fact as well as in name last Monday, succeeding Mrs. Anna R. Nichols, immediately appointed her county school board of education, naming A. C. Kellogg, Grandview; Mrs. Jean D. Zickler, Buena; Mrs. Elizabeth Bell, Yakima; and F. L. Sincock. Mrs. Zickler was a member of Mrs. Nichols' board, and is a member of the state examination board, as well as nutrition project leader of the county. .

Continuing the good work carried on by the previous administration. Miss Clark intends to do all she can to further the continuation of the community work among patrons of the different school districts in the county. To do this, she has appointed the following nineteen leaders in community work:

Whitneyville. Oct. 20th. 1938.

Dear Jessie —

As usual, I am very slow in answering your letter. When I am home, there are so many interruptions that I have a poor chance. But when I get settled in town, there is nothing to hinder me from writing. I shall be alone then most of the time. So you have parted with June, in a sense. But as she is such a home girl, you will never heed the separation you are really not separated

Whitneyville, Oct. 29th, 1938

Dear Jessie,

As usual, I am very slow in answering your letter. When I am home, there are so many interruptions that I have a poor chance. But when I get settled in town, there is nothing to hinder me from writing. I shall be alone then most of the time.

So you have parted with June, in a sense. But as she is such a home girl, you will never heed the separation.

Just weeks before this letter was written, on September 23, 1938, June and Glenn were married. Their first home was in Sedro Woolley, though they would later live in several locations around Washington State.

as Sedro - Woolley is so near. It is not at all like your mother's case. She left all and went to live in a strange country. She was lucky in having the best of husbands, which helped immensely. I received such an interesting letter from your father this week. It is over a year since I had a letter from him before. I know he is a very busy person with little spare time for writing letters. We have had some delightful weather lately, more like

and M.S. — Yes and in Canada, so busy

You are really not separated as Sedro Woolley is so near. It is not at all like your mother's case. She left all and went to live in a strange country. She was lucky in having the best of husbands, which helped immensely.

I received such an interesting letter from your father this week. It is over a year since I had a letter from him before. I know he is a very busy person with little spare time for writing letters.

This reminder of the distance that Jessie's mother lived from her own family hints again that it must have been difficult for her sister Margaret, who lived a continent away. However, it was apparently some comfort that she had a husband that they considered "the best of husbands."

early September than October.

I am planning to move into town next month if all is well. As the home folks do not use the car in the winter, they will be putting it away soon, and I want to move before they do. Otherwise, it costs me $2 to move my few belongings.

I think we were more thankful this year on Thanksgiving Day (Oct. 10th) than usual, because of the hopes of peace in Europe. It may only be for a time, because Hitler is not to be trusted. I wish it had been possible for Great Britain to say to him, "Go ahead and do your worst," but Chamberlain was not ready to sacrifice the lives of millions of young men. It is such a dirty trick of the 'yellow press' in Great Britain and US. — Yes and in Canada, to say

We have had some delightful weather lately, more like early September than October.

I am planning to move into town next month if all is well. As the home folks do not use the car in the winter, they will be putting it away soon, and I want to move before they do. Otherwise, it costs me $2. to move my few belongings.

I think we were more thankful this year on Thanksgiving Day (Oct. 10th) than usual, because of the hopes of peace in Europe. It may only be for a time, because Hitler is not to be trusted. I wish it had been possible for Great Britain to say to him, "Go ahead and do your worst." But Chamberlain was not ready to sacrifice the lives of millions of young men. It is such a dirty trick of the "yellow press" in Great Britain and US – yes and in Canada, to say that Chamberlain was cowardly.

When it came to the time when war was imminent in twenty-four hours – I think Chamberlain deserves the thanks of the civilized world. Even German women have written letters of thanks to him for preventing war. The truth of the matter is gradually becoming known to the public. France _would_ _not_ go to the help of the Czechs although she was pledged to do so. England had never made any promises to do so. It was France that urged that the matter be settled without war.

That Chamberlain was cowardly. When it came to the time when war was imminent in twenty-four hours—I think Chamberlain deserves the thanks of the civilized world. Even German women have written letters of thanks to him for preventing war. The truth of the matter is gradually becoming known to the public. France _would_ _not_ go to the help of the Czechs although she was pledged to do so. England had never made any promises to do so. It was France that urged that the matter be settled without war. We are thankful that it was

Margaret defended Neville Chamberlain, prime minister of Great Britain for his part in the Munich Agreement, signed by Britain, France, Italy, and Germany, which allowed Hitler's Germany to annex the part of Czechoslovakia known as The Sudetenland. They felt this appeasement of Germany would allow for peace in Europe. Though they may have agreed with the best of intentions, it did not stop the coming war. Margaret is right that France had an alliance with Czechoslovakia that they did not honor, though the Czechs also felt betrayed by Great Britain. History would prove the Munich Agreement to be unsuccessful, as Hitler had annexed the remainder of Czechoslovakia by the following March and invaded Poland in September, thus precipitating World War II. The Munich Agreement had, however, given hope for a short time, and Margaret was one who held onto that hope.

The "New York Times", the greatest American newspaper eulogized Chamberlain to the highest degree. The opposing political parties in England are doing much harm to the success of the peace movement. They have cheap politicians there as we have in America (Thus endeth my speech). I received a long interesting letter from Mrs Atkinson, She is a wonderful letter-writer for her age

We are thankful that it was The New York Times, the greatest American newspaper eulogized Chamberlain to the highest degree. The opposing political parties in England are doing much harm to the success of the peace movement. They have cheap politicians there as we have in America. (Thus endeth my speech).

I received a long interesting letter from Mrs. Atkinson. She is a wonderful letter-writer for her age.

She and her sister are moving into the house left them by their brother, and will sell Mrs. A's home. I always try to write her a very "proper" letter, because she sends it to England for her sister to read.

Is Billy home now or does he work away from home? I would love to peep in at you all, but that time will probably never come again.

Margaret asked if Jessie's son, Bill Pulver, was still living at home. He was twenty-one at this time and worked in the logging industry, on the trains that hauled the logs out of the woods. This would result in Bill's lifelong interest in steam locomotives.

visit are quite fresh in my mind.

Mr. and Mrs. Will Ingram are still here. They plan to return to Vancouver soon. The home folks are in their usual health. I am feeling pretty well this fall. Just before I started your letter, I made some doughnuts. Come in for your cup of coffee to-morrow morning!

Love to all the family. Is Rude at home? I suppose all his fall work is done. Do you keep chickens? I must close this empty letter.

Yours lovingly, Aunt Margaret

Margaret mentioned her last visit to Burlington, and records indicate that the visit would have been in 1928 when she visited her sister for the last time. Newspapers of that time usually had much news of local small town events, such as church meetings or luncheons. Margaret's name can be found, with her sister's, in this article from October 13, 1928.

> Friday afternoon Mrs. Herbert Hannaford entertained with a 1 o'clock luncheon in honor of her mother. Her guests included Mrs. W. H. Whitney, Miss Dunnett, Mrs. Mary Norris, Miss Grace Norris, Mrs. Nell Munro, Mrs. J. A. Walker, Miss William Leatherwood, Mrs. Rudolph Pulver and the guest of honor.

In addition to Margaret and her mother, Mrs. W.H. Whitney, Jessie was in attendance (or perhaps her mother-in-law, whose husband had the same name).

Jessie's last letter of the 1930's was written by her Aunt Marjorie, Margaret and Jane Dunnet's youngest sister. It is evident in this letter that she very seldom wrote to Jessie, and perhaps this was even the first time.

Sunny Corner   Dec. 31, 1939

Dear Jessie:

I think that I had better write you a letter to-day if I write this year, as this seems to be the last day of the year.

Well Jessie I intended to write to you often, but neglected doing so, but better late than never.

How did you folks enjoy Xmas. I hope Santa was good to you.

We certainly had a lovely Xmas day, not much snow, and so bright and sunny.

We did not have all our family home with us.

all about them. First Rose is the oldest of the family and she is married to Ross Mullin and she lives quite handy home. She has seven of a family. The eldest is a girl and her name is Avis. and the youngest is nearly three. She has just one boy about sixteen years old. Her husband is working down in St John(your father will know where that is) and Avis went down there yesterday to work too.

Then Weldon is next in our family, he lives near us too. he is married and has two girls, and Harvey is married, but has no family. Then Jean is married to an Allison and has two boys.

Then Ernest is married and lives in Montreal and they have no children.

And Wesley lives home here with us he is married, and they have one little girl, four years old. And last but not least is Merle she is nineteen, y she just finished school in June. She is talking about going in to train for a nurse, but in those small hospitals, it is quite hard to get a chance.

So that is our family. I know you will get them all mixed up. when I did not write before. You know Rose is,

I will tell you all about them. First Rose is the oldest of the family and she is married to Ross Mullin and she lives quite handy home. She has seven of a family. The eldest is a girl and her name is Avis, and the youngest is nearly three. She has just one boy - about sixteen years old. Her husband is working down in St. John (Your father will know where that is) and Avis went down there yesterday to work too.

Then Weldon is next in our family, he lives near us too. He is married and has two girls and Harvey is married, but has no family. Then Jean is married to an Allison and has two boys.

Then Ernest is married and lives in Montreal and they have no children.

And Wesley lives home here with us. He is married, and they have one little girl, four years old. And last but not least is Merle she is *nineteen, she just finished school in June. She is talking about going in to train for a nurse, but in those small hospitals, it is quite hard to get a chance.*

So that is our family. I know you will get them all mixed up when I did not write before. You know Rose is named for your mother. I must try and get a snap of her and send you.

Jessie's Aunt Marjorie is introducing Jessie's first cousins to her by way of this letter. It's apparent that Jessie had not met them, and she probably never did.

I live about five miles from Whitneyville, up in Sunny Corner and across the Miramichi River is a bridge right handy to our house and Red Bank is across the river.

We have three churches, and two Halls quite handy and plenty of dances in the summer, if that is any good. Merle likes to dance so well, but I don't like too many of them.

I was down to your Uncle Ed's not long ago. They are all fine there now, but your Aunt Margaret has been poorly lately...

She looked good this summer, but she is quite thin, and not much to build on. But I phoned to her yesterday, and she said that she felt some better.

Your Uncle Bob's daughter Margaret went to Montreal Friday, she is training for a nurse in the Miramichi Hospital in Newcastle, so they have to go to Montreal to take six months course in children's work and other work. He has one girl home with him.

I think you will have to come home here and see all your relations for you have quite a few among the Whitneys and Dunnets. I know that you would enjoy yourself in the summer of course in the winter there is a lot of snow sometimes, but not as much here as there used to be in your father's time.

It would be lovely if your father could come back here and see the folks. Of course most of his companions and people have gone.

Well, I must close my letter for it is supper time.

Write as soon as you can. Wishing you all a Happy New Year.

With love, Aunt Marjorie

yourself. in the summer of course
in the winter, there is a lot of
snow sometimes, but not as much
here as there used to be in your
father's time
          It would be lovely if you
father, could come back here
and see the folks. of course
most of his companions and old
people have gone.
          Well I must close my
letter for it is supper time.
          Write as soon as you can
Wishing you all a Happy
          New Year.
With love,   Aunt Marjorie

Chapter 5

The 1940's began with a new baby, Jessie's first grandchild, Glenda. June and Glenn became the proud parents of Glenda June Gee, born June 29, 1940. Jessie's Aunt Margaret took an interest in the baby and wrote of her often, both to Jessie and June. During this decade, all seven of Jessie's grandchildren were born, five of them to Bill and two to June.

World War II dominated the news at this time, and Margaret kept up on that and passed on her Canadian perspective.

Newcastle, March 28th, 1940

Dear Jessie,

Conscience or some other influence keeps reminding me day after day, that I must write to you. On a day that I have a little extra to do, my hand is not very steady, so I keep putting off my letters.

I was so sorry to hear, through June's letter, that Rude had been injured. I do hope that he is as "good as new" now. You must have been worried. Yesterday, I had a very pleasant surprise when I took a letter out of my box and saw your father's writing on the envelope. How well he writes! As usual, it was a very interesting letter. I must write to him soon.

It must be gratifying to him that he is able to carry on every day. Work is a blessing (if it is not too strenuous). My little bit of housekeeping keeps me fairly busy. The only cooking, except my meals, are doughnuts, biscuits, and an occasional bran cake for health. I always try to have a hearty dinner. Breakfast, if I have coffee and doughnuts, is quite satisfying. I do not try to eat a hearty supper, as it does not agree with me.

*I have quoted this backwards. *Spring is "lingering in the lap of *winter". We had some cold stormy weather around Easter. I had planned to go up home to spend the holidays, but the snow-storm blocked traffic altogether. The home folks did not get any mail for four days.*

The noon meal was commonly called dinner, and the evening meal was supper in this time period, especially in farming communities. A heavier noon meal was necessary for many because of the manual labor done in the afternoon.

Easter fell on March 24th in 1940, so that was late for a snow-storm that made streets impassable and mail impossible to deliver.

The Streets now are covered with slush and dirty snow, and walking is difficult. But spring is coming!!

What is the news from Anna Nichols? Poor Anna! What a queer life she has had! Instead of a comfortable home of her own, she had to earn her living. Auntie Rogers left her plenty .

I suppose you see June quite often. Her last letter was very interesting. What a womanlly person she is! I do enjoy the little confidences, such as her preparations for the "blessed event". As I grow older, I do appreciate the attentions of younger people, and children. If you were to walk downtown with me you would hear"Hello! Aunt Margaret" from some children who are not at all related. I enjoy this.

I must write Etta and Rosamond soon. Etta really owes me a letter, but what is an extra letter between relatives?

Jessie and Etta are pictured together here.

Does Etta go through life in a hurry? She always seemed so energetic. Your father said that he expected Bill Whitney up soon, also that Bill Forsyth dropped in occasionally. I liked him and his family very much.

Katherine is still in New York, isn't she? A Newcastle girl, a relative of some of Katherine's relatives, met her in N.Y. They decided that the world was small, after all.

Isn't the war situation rather puzzling? For a week now, no Allied ship has been sunk, but the neutral countries have suffered severely in the loss of ships and lives. Do you suppose that madman, Hitler is trying to force these neutrals to declare war on him? Sweden seems too scared. If she had allowed the Allies to go through her country, Finland might have been saved, but who knows! The end seems a long way off. With kindest regards to all the clan, I remain, Yours lovingly, Aunt Margaret

Newcastle, April 16th, 1940

Dear Jessie –

Do I owe you a letter? I am always in a state of indebtedness to my friends for letters. You would be surprised at the number of letters I get in spite of my neglect. To-day I received four, two of them from Scotland. One of them, from a cousin in the north, was opened by the censor, the first to have this done to a letter since war started. Caithness (the land of our forefathers) is in the restricted area. No visitors are allowed to visit that part of Scotland. Only Pentland Firth separates it from the Orkneys and Shetlands which the Germans seem to have such a desire to destroy.

Hitler's last outrage – invading Norway – seems to be the "last straw". Well, he is getting more than he bargained for there, according to radio and newspaper reports. The end is far off, I fear. Although my cousins' letter was opened by the censor, she did not even mention war, air raids, or even her relatives who are in the force. Her nephew is in the Air Force "somewhere in Britain". Secrecy is ordered everywhere. When the ship "Queen Elizabeth" sailed in full view down the river Clyde not a word was mentioned in any newspaper until she was in port in New York. Don't say that the Scotch are not "tight-lipped!"

Have I written to you since I had a short visit up home? The roads now are almost impassable, the bus cannot run, and there is no railroad up to that part of the country. Your Uncle Ed was down on Monday in the home car which is a light one. They managed without getting stuck in the mud. The ice has not yet gone out of the river.

I got a spring hat, but do not like it. I am returning it. Hats are so freakish, I find it hard to get one suitable for an old dame like me. This is a badly scribbled letter. The neuritis in my hands is always worse on the day I wash. My wash is not big, but I have to wring by hand. In about six weeks time, I shall probably be moving out of town. Hope you are all well. Love to all. Yours lovingly, Aunt Margaret

P.S. I wonder if I owe June a letter. I probably do.

World War II had been raging for about six months at this time if one considers Hitler's invasion of Poland, on September 1, 1939, as the beginning of the war. Margaret was correct in her fear that the end was far off as the war would not officially end until six years later.

Margaret's sense of humor shows up here with her comments about hats being "freakish" and not suitable for an "old dame." Margaret was seventy-four at this time.

Whitneyville. July 4ᵗʰ, 1940

Dear Jessie -

This is your big day, just as ours was on Monday. I could not celebrate very well - just hung out some flags.

I have been watching every mail for news from Sedro Woolley. June's last letter was mailed June 14th, and she said that I might look for news anytime. So far, none came.

Your strawberries are done now, and ours are only beginning. We had our first last night at supper. June has been a cold wet month. July is keeping up the wet record. It is raining hard to-day.

Margaret refers to Dominion Day, a Canadian holiday that commemorates the uniting of three provinces to become one country, Canada, on July 1, 1867. In 1982 the name of the holiday was changed to Canada Day. Even though Canada was an independent country, Britain kept limited control, which was not completely released until 1982. Margaret seemed to feel very proud of the strong connection with Britain, making many references to England and its place in the world.

The news Margaret refers to from Sedro Woolley was the birth of June's baby, Jessie's first grandchild. Glenda June Gee was born on June 29, 1940, but news traveled more slowly back in the 40's, so Margaret would not have received the news at the time she wrote the letter.

up the wet record. It is
raining hard to-day.
Yesterday, I received a letter
from my cousin in the north
of Scotland. Seven lines were
rubbed out by the censor who
opened it. I think she told me
something about an air raid.
When air raids are mentioned
over the radio, such expressions
as "north-east" or north-west
of Scotland," or the same of
England are ~~mentioned~~ used.
The Germans over-reached
themselves when they torpedoed
the boat carrying German and
Italian prisoners to Canada. Well,

Yesterday, I received a letter from my cousin in the north of Scotland. Seven lines were rubbed out by the censor who opened it. I think she told me something about an air raid. When air raids are mentioned over the radio such expressions as "north-east or north-west of Scotland", or the same of England are used. The Germans over-reached themselves when they torpedoed the boat carrying German and Italian prisoners to Canada.

Well, we won't have to feed them now. That sounds hard, doesn't it? But when they take such fiendish pleasure in killing women and children, nothing is too bad to say about them. We need the food to feed all the little refugees who are coming. 100,000 are expected. I wish I had money enough to take some of the poor little children. There will be many wet pillows for a while. Just think of a child of five or six having to leave parents and come to a strange land. They will need a lot of love to help make up.

Margaret did admit to sounding "hard" as she showed no sympathy for the German and Italian POW's who were killed by torpedo on their way to POW camps in Canada. In general, though, prisoners of war from Europe were treated well in Canada during World War II. They helped on farms and with logging. Some even returned to Canada, after the war, to make their homes there.

Though it was planned that 100,000 British children would be sent to Canada, actually much fewer were sent. Some parents made private arrangements, and the government sent some to Canada, the US, and some of the dominions (such as South Africa and Australia). Because of the sinking of two ships carrying evacuees, including children, the government cut back on the program. Many children were sent to the countryside of England to live with host families for a few months or for up to six years.

Margaret's love for children is demonstrated here with her wish to be able to "take some of the poor little children." Her empathy for their situation also comes through in this letter.

Very few articles have gone up in price, but the taxes are heavy. What do you think of Henry Ford's attitude? People talk of boycotting Ford cars, but you can't keep a good Ford down, can you? But he could be, at least, grateful to Great Britain for keeping the seas free for neutral ships, as far as can be done.

I forgot Etta's birthday until it was too late to send by ordinary mail, so I sent a card by airmail. Hope she gets it in time. How is your father these times? I have not had a letter from him for a long time. Mrs. Atkinson writes regularly, and likes to mention him and the family.

Here Margaret talks of Henry Ford's political leanings. She may have been referring to his being one of the most famous of Hitler's foreign backers and the award he received from the Nazis in the 1930's. Ford profited from both sides in World War II.

In this letter, as in others, Margaret discussed the world situation in one paragraph and then went to family business, including Etta's birthday. During Margaret's two visits to Burlington, she had stayed long enough to make friends there. Presumably, Mrs. Atkinson is such a friend.

What a loyal friend she is! I have not heard from Anna Nichols since Christmas. I wrote to her and addressed the letter to Yakima, care of her daughter. If she is not there, I suppose the letter will be forwarded to her.

I am glad that you see the Forsyths once in a while. I liked the family. His people live within sight of this house and Sunday night, I saw his mother and three sisters at church. His mother is eighty-eight, I think.

Once in a while, I meet your Uncle Fred. He looks pretty well this summer.

Anna Nichols and the Forsyths were relatives of Margaret and Jessie. Margaret's mother was a Forsyth (though it is unclear how these Forsyths were related to her). Anna Nichols was Margaret's cousin on her mother's side.

Uncle Fred. He looks pretty well this summer.

I wish you could come east some time and meet your relatives on both sides of the house. I have not seen your Aunt Marjorie lately, but often talk with her over the phone. She and family are well. I have not been up there yet for a visit as the weather has been very wet.

Kathleen's husband is away for the summer months with a party on a government survey. She is staying now with her father and mother. As your Aunt May is not very well at times, she

I wish you could come east some time and meet your relatives on both sides of the house. I have not seen your Aunt Marjorie lately, but often talk with her over the phone. She and family are well. I have not been up there yet for a visit as the weather has been very wet.

Kathleen's husband is away for the summer months with a party on a government survey. She is staying now with her father and mother. As your Aunt May is not very well at times, she likes to have Kathleen with her.

Uncle Fred was Jessie's father's younger brother. Aunt Marjorie was Margaret's younger sister. Kathleen was Margaret's brother Edward's daughter. Aunt May was Edward Dunnet's wife.

So now there are four women in this house. Ernest's wife is here too. I keep out of the way most of the time. But when doughnuts are to be made I am generally useful. It is a busy job, and makes lots of dirty dishes which I always wash.

Now I must close this poor letter. Love to all the clan.

Yours lovingly, Aunt Margaret

Congratulations to Grandma and Grandpa Pulver! I planned to write some time ago, but kept putting off until I could get rid of my attack of neuritis. It is still with me, however. Everybody admires the card June sent announcing the birth of the baby. It is one of the prettiest I have ever seen. I sent one of congratulations by air. Since then I received such a nice letter from June telling me more about the baby. I must write to her soon. I am glad that she is well. Your Uncle Bob's son Nelson lives near him. Yesterday a little daughter arrived to his house.

They are naming her "Kathleen June". No one around here bears the name of June. "Kathleen" is for your Uncle Ed's daughter, Frances. Nelson's wife likes the name of June very much. This is their second child – the eldest is a boy named "Shirley." Robert Shirley is his full name.

her "Kathleen June". No one around here bears the name of June. "Kathleen" is for your Uncle Ed's daughter, Frances. Nelson's wife likes the name of June very much. This is their second child — the eldest is a boy named "Shirley". Robert Shirley is his full name. What a beaten track will be seen from Burlington to Sedro-Woolley! A baby is a strong magnet! When I was in Newcastle, I usually stopped the baby-carriages to have a look at their occupants — some pretty, and some not, but all so sweet. When children are about two or three, I have quite a following. I call myself the "Pied Piper". They

What a beaten track will be seen from Burlington to Sedro-Woolley! A baby is a strong magnet. When I was in Newcastle, I usually stopped the baby-carriages to have a look at their occupants - some pretty, and some not, but all so sweet. When children are about two or three, I have quite a following. I call myself the "Pied Piper".

Sedro Woolley is where June and Glenn lived and is about five miles from Burlington, so it was a short trip for Jessie to drive to see her granddaughter. Margaret had close contact with Kathleen and Shirley and mentioned them frequently in her letters over the years. They were her niece and nephew.

They follow me around even if I do not "pipe". One little fellow followed me down town one day, and I had to turn and take him back. That has happened more than once. Was I pleased! Yes, indeed. I do love the little ones. I am sorry that I shall never see little "Glenda June", unless she comes to see me soon.

Now for a favor – could you find out from your father, without letting him know I asked you, whether he received the little parcel of maple sugar I sent him. I insured the parcel. I sent some last year and did not hear whether he got it or not. The post office clerk asked me to let her know. She said that owing to its contents, it might be stolen. We old people do not want to admit that we sometimes forget ...

...so do not give me away. It is a small thing to worry about anyway, but I do want him to get the sugar. Perhaps I could mail it from some other P.O. next time.

What have you heard from Anna Nichols? I wrote to her this summer, but got no reply.

We have had quite a number of summer visitors, chiefly from the USA. Last week we had some from Maine.

So President Roosevelt is offering for a third term. As he seems so favorable towards Great Britain, the only country now left to put down the <u>Beast</u> we hope he will be elected. I think he will help with everything except actual warfare. Man power is really not needed just now.

Kindest regards to the clan.

Lovingly,

Aunt Margaret

Margaret inquired again about Anna Nichols. In a letter to June, earlier in 1940, she had asked, "What is the news from Anna Nichols? I have not written lately, because I was afraid she could not read a letter." So something had happened to Anna Nichols, who was sixty-five years old. Anna died, two years later, on March 19, 1942.

Margaret referred to Hitler as the Beast in her letter and, though she did not expect the US to join in the war, she thought Roosevelt would be helpful to the Allied cause. Of course, he would prove helpful to the cause. However, he would not officially declare war until 1941. He remained neutral for the first two years of the conflict. Though being officially neutral, the US did provide war materials to China, Russia, and Great Britain through the Lend Lease Program.

Once again, Margaret expressed concern about the delivery of a package. One wonders if she really had so little faith in the postal system, or if she was just hoping to get a letter of thanks that she had not received.

These are the only letters to Jessie from Margaret in 1940, and they do not resume until 1944. There are, however, letters from Margaret to Jessie's daughter, June. In December of 1940, Margaret wrote that her brother, Robert, was very ill and that his daughter, Kathleen, had been sent to bed for six months because it was presumed she had tuberculosis. In February of 1941, Margaret wrote:

Since I received your letter, we have all had some sorrowful days. My brother, Robert, who has not been well for quite some time, became much worse, and gone to the hospital here for examination and treatment. The x-ray showed a growth at the base of his lungs; the blood-test showed that he was anemic, and besides his heart was weak. So after a few weeks of suffering, he passed away on Jan. 18th. He could not lie down, night or day. Had to be pillowed up high on account of his breathing. Had he lived longer, he would have suffered more, so we were thankful that he was spared that. We miss him ever so much. Two weeks before he died I went up to see him.

Margaret also refers to Marguerite, Robert's daughter who had been treated for TB.

"Marguerite is getting along pretty well. Her father's death set her back some, but she is improving. She hopes to have another x-ray at the end of this month. Perhaps she will not need to stay in bed the full six months. This is the year that she hoped to graduate.

Tuberculosis was still a dreaded disease in the early 1940's and was treated in much the same way it had been when Jessie had TB in 1918. By the later 1940's TB was treated with antibiotics, and people did not have lengthy periods of bed rest.

In more family news, Margaret told June that Jessie's cousin, Jean Dunnet, had gotten married, though she didn't get a chance to go to the ceremony. She said, "Jean's wedding dress and hat were blue." In 1943, Margaret wrote that Jessie's cousin's son, Melvin Dunnet, was to graduate in Agriculture and

Manual Training from Harkins Academy in Newcastle, where Margaret had taught for so many years. Another cousin, Jean Dunnet, had graduated from there the previous year and was now working in an office in Ottawa and graduating from a commercial course. "What wonderful opportunities young people have these days!" Margaret wrote.

Four generations are represented here: June Pulver Gee, Jessie Whitney Pulver, Glenda Gee, and William Hiram Whitney.

In June of 1944, Jessie received the following letter from her Aunt Margaret.

Whitneyville, June 16th, 1944

Dear Jessie,

Do I owe you a letter? My relatives and friends have been taking second place lately, as "my boys" overseas must get their letters promptly. It means so much to them to hear their names called out when mail arrives. One boy wrote me that nothing helped the morale of the soldiers' more than getting letters. Some of them alas! are in the thick of the fight now in France. June wrote to me that Billy is now a prisoner. When I heard that he had gone overseas, I wrote Faye and Bill for his address, then when I heard that he was listed as "missing", I wrote a letter of sympathy and sent it air mail, but received no reply to either of them.

Jessie's nephew, Bill, was taken prisoner during World War II. He was captured on April 27, 1944 when the plane he was co-piloting was shot down by Germans over France. It was his first combat mission and, after being shot down, he hid in a hay shock waiting for dark. He was, however, discovered by dogs the Germans were using to track him down. Another pilot who had seen the plane crash thought that Bill had died instantly and wrote to his parents to say that. Bill was ultimately held as a prisoner of war in St. Omer, France and then in Germany.

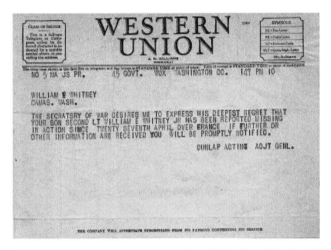

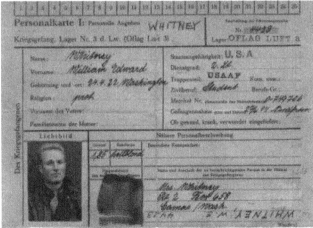

Portion of prisoner file card maintained by Germans
Card originated May 6, 1944

I asked them to let me know if they got any other news. June set my mind at rest when I got her letter a few days ago. What a good letter she writes! Inherited, I am sure. How are your crops coming on? June has been a very cool month here. One morning this week we woke up to find the ground covered with frost. This morning is cool enough to enjoy a fire.

I received a letter from Mrs. Atkinson recently – two in fact, the last one having ten pages. As she had not heard from me lately, she imagined I was sick. She mentioned having written to you and Etta. She still loves to get Burlington news. I wrote to her this week and told her that I would put her on my over-seas list, and she might get a letter oftener.

It is unclear who Mrs. Atkinson was, but it seems odd by today's standards that Margaret would call a friend Mrs. Atkinson, rather than by her first name. They must have been fairly good friends if they corresponded so frequently and the letters were of such length.

Jessie with her grandchildren in the mid-1940's. She is holding Loren and Jeanne; in front are Steve, Patty, and Glenda.

Your Aunt Marjorie's husband is getting much weaker. He is now in bed. We were up to see him on Sunday. They live about four miles farther up the river, and we can easily go there.

Kathleen and her husband have a position in Loggieville, at the Terminal Hotel. L. is about twenty miles farther down the river. We went down to see them on Wednesday evening, and enjoyed our trip very much. It was the first time your Aunt May had been there. Kathleen does not like to live alone, so she usually gets something to do where her husband works.

Marguerite, your Uncle Bob's daughter is now a nursing sister with the rank of 2nd Lieut. After six months, she will be a 1st.

Marjorie was married to Perley Tozer, and both of them died that year, 1944.

> *now stationed at Petawawa Ontario. The Military Hospital there has four hundred beds. and the Camp is the second largest in Canada. She would love to be posted on the Pacific Coast or overseas, since she cannot be in New Brunswick. She spent her 48 hr. leave in Montreal lately, with her old friend Ruth Whitney (Hiram's daughter) Your father will recognize the latter name. Probably I told you all this before. I write so many letters that I get slightly mixed occasionally.*
>
> *I am enclosing a clipping about a former pupil of mine, and also a relative of ours. His mother and your mother were first cousins. He has been very nice to me for both reasons. He sent me a lovely gift at Christmas*

She is now stationed at Petawawa Ontario. The Military Hospital there has four hundred beds, and the camp is the second largest in Canada. She would love to be posted on the Pacific Coast or overseas, since she cannot be in New Brunswick. She spent her 48 hour leave in Montreal lately, with her old friend Ruth Whitney (Hiram's Daughter). Your father will recognize the latter name. Probably I told you all this before - I write so many letters that I get slightly mixed occasionally.

I am enclosing a clipping about a former pupil of mine, and also a relative of ours. His mother and your mother were first cousins. He *has been very nice to me for both reasons.*

He sent me a lovely gift at Christmas and since he returned to Ponoka, he sent me two rolls of films for my camera. He knows I have a hobby for taking pictures. His sister invited me down to have dinner with him while he was visiting her.

Among my former pupils, I have six doctors. I call them my "honor roll". One of them was my doctor when I had the "flu" last winter; therefore I had no bill to pay.

The prospects for a strawberry crop are practically "nil". The ice during the winter, and the late frost, have injured the plants. It is reported that for the province, it will be as low as 60%. Your Uncle Ed still goes full steam ahead. It is nice to see him so well.

My Maine friends are still urging me to come this summer...

Margaret kept in touch with many of her former students and showed pride in their accomplishments. There are several examples in her letters of generous gifts from her former students, from cash for travel to free medical care.

Jessie's Uncle Ed, her mother's brother, would have been seventy-six years old at this time. He lived until May of 1947.

I have taken the first step in getting ready to cross the border - passport photos. But the birth certificate will prove a "snag". When I arrived on this sphere, it was such an unimportant event, that I was not registered. Birth registration did not become law until 1920. I have to get a health check-up, not for immigration purposes, but to see if the long bus trip would not be good for me with a poor engine, (mine, not the bus's.) Have not had my usual pep since I had the "flu". This letter seems to be all about myself. Put all errors down to old age weaknesses. Write me when you can. Love to all your family, including Bill,

Vera and children. What a big boy Stevie is now!

During World War II restrictions on border crossing between Canada and the US seem to have reverted to something similar to restrictions during World War I. Following World War II, restrictions eased, but after the bombing of the World Trade Center on September 11, 2001, it tightened again, so that a passport is now required.

June sent me a snap of him with Glenda. I would love to see your three grandchildren. What a joy they must be to you! Your father no doubt, enjoys his great-grandchildren - 5 of them, very much. I have not had a letter from him for a long time. Please give my kind regards to Blanche Crossley when you see her. Is her married name La Thorp? I do not feel sure, so could not send her a card at Christmas.

Please show Etta this clipping and explain when you see her. She wrote me when Billy W. was missing, and sent me a clipping from the paper.

Now I must stop, so that this letter will get mailed to-day. Hoping you and Rude are well, I remain yours lovingly, Aunt Margaret

In August of 1944, Margaret told June, in a letter, that she had taken her first airplane ride.

I traveled from Bangor to Houlton by plane, a distance of 120 miles in less than an hour. It was my first flight, therefore, a thrilling experience. My cousin gave me the ticket. He said that he would get much pleasure in boasting that he had a cousin, 78 years of age, who took her first flight. Climbing to 4,000 feet, the distance the plane usually takes, made my ears crack, but that passed away after a while. The going was very smooth except when we struck a "pocket". Then the plane seemed to drop a few feet, and my stomach did too, just like coming down in an elevator too swiftly. The landing was perfect. Don't be surprised if I fly to the Pacific Coast, ha-ha. Now that I have started, I would not hesitate to take another trip, providing someone gave me the ticket.

Margaret began to worry that when she passed on, there would no longer be any correspondence between the Washington State and New Brunswick relatives. At one point, she wrote to June:

I hope when I am gone, that some of the younger ones will take up the correspondence. The only one, who might do so, is Margaret Dunnet, my niece.

Jessie's first three
granddaughters,
Glenda, Patty, and Jeanne.

Whitneyville, Nov. 5th, 1944

Dear Jessie,

This is only a line to tell you that your Aunt Marjorie passed away very suddenly last Tuesday night from a heart attack. She was not very well all summer. She went to Saint John in August to visit her daughter. While there she had a heart attack. She came home over a month ago, when she had another one, quite severe. The doctor sent her to bed for two weeks.

She then felt much better, and was able to go around and do light jobs. I went up to see her on Tuesday afternoon, and found her much better, but the attack came on that evening, and she passed away in half an hour. It was a great shock to us all, and especially to her family. Their father died only four months ago. All came home to the funeral except one son in Montreal. Later on, I will send you, Etta, and your father the local papers.

I have not felt like writing before. I never dreamed that she or your mother would go before I did. There are now only your Uncle Ed and I left of a family of ten.

Had one of June's lovely letters and yours with snaps in them. The "four" generation picture is fine.

Lovingly, Aunt Margaret

P.S. Address for winter – Newcastle. Plan to move this week. Just as soon as I can get some prints, I will send you a snap of your Aunt M.

Margaret was the oldest sibling who had lived beyond the

first few years of childhood; the first three children had died before they reached five years of age. Her sister Marjorie was twelve years younger, so it is understandable that Margaret did not expect to outlive her. Marjorie was sixty-six years old at the time of her death.

In 1945 there are no letters to Jessie, but there are several to June. In one of them Margaret talks about a new outfit she had made.

A dress that fits my bust and hips – 32, is not nearly long enough. I dislike seeing old dames in their seventies wearing skirts up to the knees, but it is the style, *however.*

Margaret also talked about the travels of Jessie's cousin Marguerite, who was a nurse, listing all the places she had visited in Scotland while stationed in England. Margaret mentioned that she had been one of the last nurses posted overseas during World War II. In other war news, Margaret said she would probably not be going to Maine that year, as traveling was difficult because of all the troops coming home. "How happy the Whitney family must be over Billy's return!" she stated.

Newcastle, Nov.24th, 1946

Dear Jessie,

How are all my Pacific Coast relatives? I have had only one letter from that region since early in the summer, and that one was
from your dad. Even June, my most faithful correspondent, has not
written for a long time. Of course, with her two children, she is a
busy woman. She writes a very interesting letter. Since I moved to
town - October 10th, I have been very busy. First of all, my landlady had to go to bed with an acute attack of phlebitis. I cooked and
carried her meals; looked after the house, in a manner, so I was
pretty busy. When she got better I took a few days off and went to
Fredericton to visit some sick friends. These friends expected me to
visit them on my way home from Bangor, Maine, but I came home

by a different route, by plane from Bangor to Moncton.

This journey, by rail would have taken from four o'clock in the morning until three in the afternoon. The plane took only one hour and twenty minutes. I enjoyed the flight ever so much. The day was sunny and flying conditions of the best. We did not strike one "pocket". This was on a Saturday afternoon. I stayed with my nephew and his wife until Monday morning, and came to Newcastle by train. There is an army airport about six miles from here, but is not ready for civilian traffic.

I was in the USA for three months. When I got home, I found your Uncle Ed in very poor health. He is not allowed to work anymore - has a heart condition.

It appears that two years after her first flight, Margaret flew again. Jessie, however, lived her entire life without ever having a plane ride. Her travels were very limited compared to Margaret's.

His daughter and her husband are taking care of him, and her mother, who is quite lame.

We have no snow yet. It is getting much colder, so we shall soon have some. October and much of November have been delightful - sunny nearly every day. Did you see the eclipse yesterday? It was a great sight - about 70% covered. The part of the sun not covered reminded me of a new moon - crescent-shaped. I used some old films to look through.

Haven't you a new granddaughter? Do write me about her. Love to

Bill, Vera, June and family and Rude. Hope you are all well. I must write your dad and Etta.

Lovingly, Aunt Margaret

P.S. My landlady is in bed again – phlebitis. She has to keep off her feet for a time. She is a large, stout person.

The granddaughter mentioned here was Joanne Nadine Pulver, Bill and Vera Pulver's fourth child.

These children are Anna Rose and William Whitney's great-grandchildren. They are gathered at Etta and Jess Burford's home in Mt. Vernon for Sunday dinner. They are back row l-r: Bobby Cushen, Steve Pulver, Susan Cushen, Glenda Gee; second row: Jeanne Pulver; first row: Loren Gee, Joanne Pulver, and Patty Pulver. The Cushen children are Etta's grandchildren.

Newcastle, March 13th, 1947

Dear Jessie,

My Christmas letters are not all answered yet, and now the birthday ones are here. Last night, I answered a letter I received Nov. 21st. It is hard to keep up with all the letters I get. There are sick, blind, lame and lonely on my list, and to these I <u>must</u> write. They all enjoy getting letters. On my list are six women, who like myself, have passed the 80th birthday. Some are 82, a year older than I am. One of these is an old school-mate. Your father would remember her, I think. She was Ariana Baker now Adams. She was a school sweetheart of your Uncle Ernest – who was killed when quite young.

Letters had become an even more important part of Margaret's life as she became older. Here she implies that the letter writing was almost an obligation with her underlined use of the word must.

She is failing mentally judging by her letters. Your father does not seem to age mentally. His letters are grand – I do like to get them. He has always kept up with world events and has such a keen knowledge of political affairs. It is sad to listen to the narrow, childish minded people, who can talk only about trifling things. Your grandmother Whitney was a very bright intelligent woman.

I had a wonderful birthday anniversary. One of my old pupils planned a dinner-party on the evening before, but the worst storm of the season came on, and I could not go. Taxis would not venture. It was post-poned until next day. There was a delicious three-tiered cake, decorated.

Jessie's paternal grandmother--Jessie Sinclair Whitney, for whom she had been named--had died in 1891 at sixty-eight years of age, five years before Jessie was born. The first Jessie had immigrated to Canada from Scotland.

The cousins in Bangor sent me some lovely flowers – tulips, daffodils, irises, and snapdragon. There was an exquisite American Beauty rose for a corsage which I wore to the party. (Vain old dame, eh?) I received thirty-five greeting cards, and many nice gifts. Surely my friends are kind to me.

In a most prominent place on my dresser are Glenda's and Loren's pictures. Jean's little boy keeps them company. He is a few weeks older than Loren.

I had a lovely birthday letter from Vera and Bill. It sent a thrill to my heart when I read their kind words. Wouldn't I love to see their children!

Jean was Margaret's niece who lived nearby.

This is Bill and Vera's family as of 1947. Two years later, another son would be added. From left in back row: Kathryn Jeanne, Patricia Rose, Steven William, and baby Joanne Nadine.

When my "ship comes home" I shall fly to Burlington. Every picture of June's children that comes sends a longing to see them. They all look so loveable. I had such a nice birthday letter from June enclosing some snaps. I wish you could see my album. There are page after page of little children. I have a page of June and Billy when quite young; now I have their children. I feel like a great-grandmother. What a lot I missed in life! But there are compensations. I have been free to see some of the world & satisfy my "itching feet", and if I had the money I would keep on seeing. Have not given up hope of crossing the Atlantic.

In today's world one can marry, have children, have a career, and travel as well. One wonders what Margaret would have thought of that possibility, and if she could indeed have enjoyed all of it had she been born a hundred years later. Nonetheless, her exclamation "What a lot I have missed in life" is a sad lament. She did hold out hope for a trip to Scotland, someday, to see the land of her ancestors.

-5-

We have had very stormy weather during the last month, but not very cold. Coal and wood have been quite sufficient to keep us warm. Poor Europe has shivered. I feel so sorry for the innocent little children, who suffer from cold and hunger. We the people of USA and Canada, have much to be thankful for. Prices for luxuries are going up, but we can get along without those. We pay 47 cts per lb. for butter, but get only 6 oz. per person in a week. Sugar is only '08, meat varies. I paid 36 cts for a small T bone steak, but it gave me two dinners. Shortening jumped 10 cts in a short time. It is now 30 cts.

People living in Europe did have many hardships after World War II devastated their countries. It was especially difficult for the British children who were sent to Canada during the war. They had lived in comfort in Canada while their families suffered in England, and then they went home to continuing hardship. It has been reported that many of them felt guilty for having easy lives in Canada while their families suffered in their home country. As usual, Margaret showed empathy for children.

Old-fashioned salt cod-fish is now 35 cts a pound. Our bay is full of these fish. Salmon, in season, is 40 and 45 cts. One of my birthday gifts was a large can of chicken (home-canned), a very welcome gift. I am still cooking and keeping house for myself. To-day my landlady invited me down town to dinner. It was corned beef and cabbage day, but I took roast beef. At this particular restaurant, they serve excellent apple pie for dessert – my favorite pie. How I am rambling on! The home folk are in their usual health.

usual health. Your cousin, Wesley Tozer (your Aunt Marjorie's son) and his wife, Hannah, are expecting a "blessed event" in early summer. They have only one child, a girl of twelve years, so all are pleased. I am trying to get a correspondence started between the younger cousins, because, when I leave this world, the connection will be lost. Love to the whole clan. Thanking you for birthday greetings, I remain Yours lovingly Aunt Margaret

P.S. I owe Bill & Faye; Bill and Vera and June — letters. Some day, I must answer such good ones. June sent two lovely snaps in her card — her children and Billy's

Your cousin, Wesley Tozer (your Aunt Marjorie's son) and his wife, Hannah are expecting a "blessed event" in early summer. They have only one child, a girl of twelve years, so all are pleased. I am trying to get a correspondence started between the younger cousins, because, when I leave this world, the connection will be lost. Love to the whole clan. Thanking you for birthday greetings, I remain Yours lovingly, Aunt Margaret.

P.S. I owe Bill & Faye, Bill and Vera and June letters. Some day, I must answer such good ones. June sent two lovely snaps in her card - her children and Billy's.

Later that year, in June of 1947, Margaret wrote to June about crossing the border into the US.

Restrictions at the border going in to USA are more severe… Last summer I had my fingerprints taken, just as if I were a criminal.

Surely that ought to insure me an easy crossing this summer. It is extremely easy for any one from the USA to come into Canada. I cannot understand all this "red tape" between friendly nations. The USA has its reasons, I suppose.

Dear Jessie –

Your letter of sympathy received this week. Many thanks for your kind words. I sent your Dad an airmail, but that was the time he was away, so you did not hear at once from me. I sent you and Etta the local paper, and to-day, I got one ready for Bill. As I had to go back to town after the funeral, and pack up for Whitneyville, I couldn't settle down to write.

The family member who had died was Margaret's brother, Ed. Edward Dunnet, born in 1868, was two years younger than Margaret. He was seventy-nine years of age at the time of his death. This must have been an especially difficult loss for

Margaret as it left her the only surviving family member of her generation, and she had lived close to most of her siblings.

We have a great many letters of sympathy to acknowledge, from over the province and the USA. Your Uncle Ed was well-known. He died in the house where he was born seventy-nine years ago, on May 24th. Now I am the only one left of a family of ten. I feel lonely. But my nieces and nephews are exceedingly kind. Your grandmother left me a home in her will, for as long as I live. Kathleen now owns the property, but my home is still secure.

I use it only a few months in summer. I lived in town since last Oct. 10th and moved up May 16th. My Maine friends wish me to come early, and the relatives in Bangor expect me. The latter are coming over for Memorial Day week-end.

You spoke of my going west by plane. If I could afford a trip, it would be by rail, as the scenery is so grand. One sees very little in a plane. The cost is very little more by plane, but I cannot manage either. My income barely keeps me.

keeps me. The cost of living has risen to great heights, while my income is stationary. But I am thankful for what I have. Probably, I shall not need it very long now. My little grand-nephew is quite a talker now. He is about three weeks older than Loren, so you know how interesting he is now. He calls me "Margie", and keeps my kisses on the back of his neck. I was over there yesterday, and he was so pleased. I taught him the word "humbug" which he thought very funny.

The cost of living has risen to great heights, while my income is stationary. But I am thankful for what I have. Probably, I shall not need it very long now.

My little grand-nephew is quite a talker now. He is about three weeks older than Loren, so you know how interesting he is now. He calls me "Margie", and keeps my kisses on the back of his neck. I was over there yesterday, and he was so pleased. I taught him the word "humbug" which he thought very funny.

Margaret would live to be ninety-three years of age, dying in August of 1959, so her money had to last another twelve years. Again, she demonstrated her affection for her many nieces and nephews and their children.

I would love to see your charming grand-children. I never saw but one of those tin-types you mentioned. Your grandmother gave it to your mother when she was here in 1913, I think. But somewhere, I think I have one taken with your Uncle Ed and myself, before she was married. We are both dressed in mourning for our father, who died in 1887. The picture is a photograph. I shall try to find it.

Jessie had an interest in genealogy and shared information, photos, and stories with her grandchildren, so it's not surprising that she had asked her Aunt Margaret about an old family photo. The photo of Ed, Margaret, and Anna Rose can be found on page15.

We find out here that Jessie's mother, Anna Rose, had gone back to her home in Canada for a visit in 1913. Jessie would have been seventeen then, while Rosamond was nine years old.

My belongings are somewhat mixed up.

Your cousin, Ernest and wife are to be home on Saturday. They have a cosy little "rent" about half-a-mile down the road. Your father knows the house- the old John Whitney place. It is said to be over a hundred years old. They like to have me visit them. Did I ever send you girls a snap I took of your Aunt Marjorie and her great grand daughter whose father was killed in Sicily?

whose father was killed in Sicily? He never saw his little daughter. If you three girls (I do not know Rosamond's address) would like one, I can easily send it, as I took the picture. A friend snapped one this winter with my fur coat and fur hat on. It is a real snow picture. Perhaps on some hot day I will send you one. Property is certainly very high

He never saw his little daughter. If you three girls (I do not know Rosamond's address) would like one, I can easily send it, as I took the picture. A friend snapped one this winter with my fur coat and fur hat on. It is a real snow picture. Perhaps on some hot day I will send you one.

Property is certainly very high in your town.

in your town. Ernest paid $450 for a double lot and several acres besides. It is not far from here. He will probably start building this year. His father meant this property for him, but his mother, to whom it was willed, is now mentally incapable of making a will. So it would have been undivided property which Ernest and his wife could not accept. No longer do we have "entail". I wish you could have come

Ernest paid $450 for a double lot and several acres besides. It is not far from here. He will probably start building this year. His father meant this property for him, but his mother, to whom it was willed, is now mentally incapable of making a will. So it would have been undivided property which Ernest and his wife could not accept. No longer do we have "entail".

It seems Jessie had told Margaret something about property prices in Burlington at that time, and they must have been higher than what people were paying in Northumberland County, N.B., as Margaret's comments indicated.

The *Merriam-Webster* definition of entail is "to restrict (property) by limiting the inheritance to the owner's lineal descendants or to a particular class thereof." This was done to keep a property intact and to keep it in the family. *The Random House Webster's Dictionary* defines entail as "to limit the passage of real property to a specified line or category of heirs." Does this mean Ernest bought some of his father's property from his mother? Ernest appears to be the son of Edward Dunnet, who died just before this letter was written.

I wish you could have come when your Uncle Ed and Aunt Marjorie were alive. Your Uncle Fred is quite spry. I saw him a few days ago. I was sorry to hear of Ernest Allison passing away. He was such a very nice young man when I saw him.

I owe Bill and Faye a letter. Someday, I hope to write to them.

Ed and Marjorie were Margaret's siblings who had died within two and a half years before this letter was written. Because the death of her brother Ed was so recent, Margaret seemed to be thinking of family more than usual in this letter. Ernest Allison was Jessie's cousin on her father's side, the son of William Hiram's sister Jessie. He died in Tacoma, Washington, at age sixty-five.

My niece, who was an army nurse overseas, thinks she will go to Vancouver this year to nurse in the Shaughnessy Veteran's Hospital. If she does, look out for her. She is as good as I am about "trailing" relatives. She tried to find all the Dunnets from "John O Groats to Land's End" when she was overseas. She visited three second cousins Marjory (Dunnet) Campbell; Margaret (Dunnet)

*McAuley; and Catherine (Dunnet) Swanson. All three write to
me. Probably I told you all this before.*

Some of the Dunnets in Scotland were the descendants of
Margaret's uncle William, the oldest son of her grandparents,
whose parents had left him in Scotland, as a two-year-old,
when they immigrated to Canada.

*I am trying to start some correspondence here between you folks
and these. If I should "drop out" suddenly, these folks could not
let you know, as they do not write to you. You will know it by the
absence of some letters. Please tell June, my faithful correspondent,
that I hope to write soon. Many letters of this length use up a lot
of "gray matter".*

Love to the clan – Lovingly, Aunt Margaret

Margaret had begun to worry about her death and that no one in her family would notify Jessie. She hoped that the next generation of Dunnets would correspond with the next generation of Jessie's family.

In September of 1947, Jessie received this postcard from Etta who was traveling with her husband, Jess, in California.

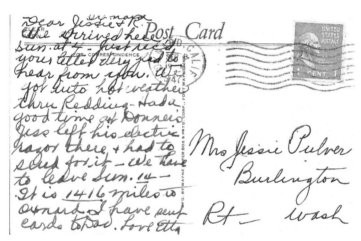

Oxnard

Dear Jessie & R. We arrived here Sun. at 4. Just rec'd your letter. Very glad to hear from you. We got into hot weather thru Redding - Had a good time at Donner's. Jess left his electric razor there & had to send for it - we have to leave Sun. 14 - It is 1416 miles to Oxnard. I have sent cards to Dad. Love Etta

The 1940's ended with the death of Jessie's husband and also her father. Rude Pulver died on June 27, 1949. Margaret wrote, in a letter to June, "Your Aunt Etta wrote me the sad news of your dear father's death. Please accept my sincere sympathy in your bereavement." This was followed, on December 17th, by the death of Jessie's father, William Whitney. After Rude's death, Jessie had moved in with her father to care for him, and she continued to live there, in her childhood home, until the last few years of her life.

Chapter 6

In the late 1940's and beyond – into the 1980's actually -- Jessie's grandchildren wrote to her. The early letters told of the everyday happenings of their families, the Gees and the Pulvers. The children expressed their love for Jessie in their letters, and it was obvious she played a significant role in their lives. They also wrote about their siblings, sometimes sharing what they were doing right at that moment. The Pulver children were Steve, Patty, Jeanne, Joanne, and Donny, who were later called Steve, Pat, Jean, Jo, and Don. They were Bill and Vera's family. Glenda and Loren were June and Glenn Gee's children.

This picture of the Pulver children was taken in August 1950.

This homemade valentine was from a grandchild who did not sign it.

Before the grandchildren could write, they scribbled letters to Jessie. The following letter is signed, on the back, by Joanne Pulver. ("Joanne" is best read with a mirror.)

The older children frequently wrote for the younger children or helped them with their letters. What they wrote about one another showed there was much affection among the siblings.

Donny wants me to help him send some valentines to some people he knows so this is from him. Love Patty

Dear Grandma, How are you? I am fine. Joanne

It appears that an older sibling wrote Joanne's name for her on this letter.

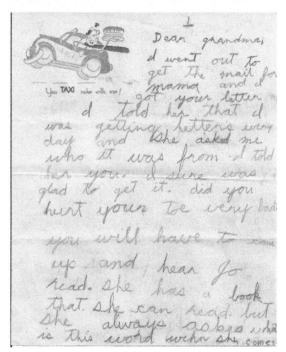

Dear Grandma, I went out to get the mail for mama and I got your letter. I told her that I was getting letters every day and she asked me who it was from. I told her you. I sure was glad to get it. Did you hurt your toe very bad?

You will have to come up and hear Jo read. She has a book that she can read, but she always asks what is this word when she comes to _look_. She says is this _look_ or _see_. Otherwise she can read good.

In that color book you got for all of us, well Jean and I made some flowers. It showed how to make them in the book. We wake up real early and color in the books.

I am starting to collect stamps. I have a different kind that I got from Nebraska. I only have two stamps.

I guess that isn't a collection yet, but it's a start anyway. I think I will ask Daddy what he is doing then I will tell you.

I asked him and he said he was fooling around, but I don't think he was though.

Steve is standing out there watching him like usual. Now I know what Daddy made. He made Mama a flower bed by the barn.

Mama and Daddy are going to kill the chickens. We are learning our times tables at school. I know some of mine but not very many. I hope you can read Jo's letter. Well I guess I don't have any more paper so Love and Kisses, Pattie My arm is tired.

Bill Pulver's family lived on Chuckanut Drive in Bellingham, on a small farm, where they raised chickens for eggs and for their Sunday dinners. The children loved to watch the killing of the chickens as they really do run around "like a chicken with its head cut off" when killed. In addition to the chickens, they raised calves for beef or to sell as veal calves, rabbits, cows, and occasionally ducks. Later, they acquired horses for the kids to ride.

I AIM TO BE YOUR VALENTINE

To Grandma
from Joe
and steve

Thursday

Dear Grandma,

how are you? mama is
better. and we are fine
this is Jean's first time
writing with InK.
I am kinda copyin
Jean. I am writing
with mama's cards
I guess you would
call them that. we
got report cards
today. I mean Jean

and Joe did. the fourth
and fifth grade had
conferences. Joe got
all s's. that means
good. But Jean got
one s - that means
not to good.
that looks like
Jo and D on on the
cover. I hope you
did what it said.
Now we have a /over

Thursday

Dear Grandma,

How are you? Mama is better, and we are fine. This is Jean's first time writing with Ink. I am kinda copying Jean. I am writing with mama's cards I guess you would call them that. We got report cards today. I mean Jean and Joe did. The fourth and fifth grade had conferences. Joe got all S's, that means good. But Jean got one S- that mean's not to good.

That looks like Jo and Don on the cover. I hope you did what it said. Now we have a (over)

...bluebird group. We have a new boy in our room at school. I'm going to try to draw a horse. Good-bye from me   Pat

Read this letter first. Don't tell Jean about that.

There was also competition among the Pulver kids. Pat, for example, wanted her letter read first, and she reported Jean's grade of S-.

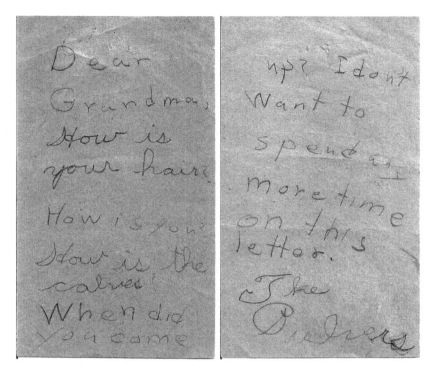

Dear Grandma,

How is your hair? How is you? How is the calves? When did you come up? I don't want to spend any more time on this letter.

The Pulvers

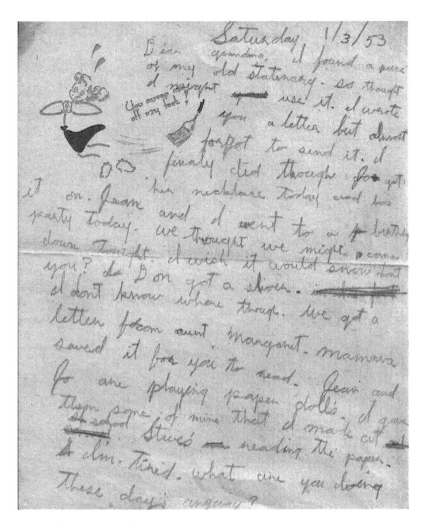

Saturday 1/3/53

Dear Grandma, I found a piece of my old stationary - so thought I might use it. I wrote you a letter but almost forgot to send it. I finally did though. Jo got her necklace today and has it on. Jean and I went to a birthday party today. We thought we might come down tonight. I wish it would snow, don't you? Don got a sliver. I don't know where though. We got a letter from Aunt Margaret. Mamma saved it for you to read. Jean and Jo are playing paper dolls. I gave them some of mine that I made at school. Steve's reading the paper. I'm tired. What are you doing these days anyway?

Pat was nine years old when she wrote this letter. The grand-children frequently sent letters to Jessie in Burlington, thirty miles away. Margaret Dunnet, Jessie's faithful correspondent in New Brunswick, is the Aunt Margaret referred to here.

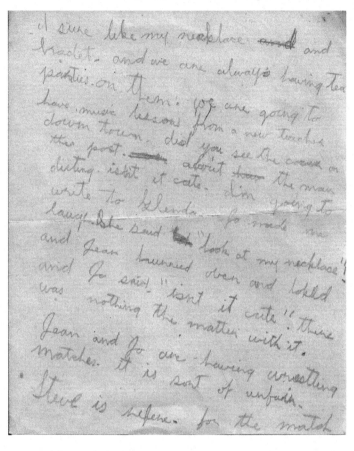

I sure like my necklace and bracelet, and we are always having tea parties in them. We are going to have music lessons from a new teacher down town. Did you see the cover on the Post about the man dieting? Isn't it cute?

I'm going to write to Glenda

Jo made me laugh. She said, "Look at my necklace!" and Jean hurried over and looked and Jo said, "Isn't it cute." There was nothing the matter with it.

Jean and Jo are having wrestling matches. It is sort of unfair. Steve is referee for the match.

The "Post" referenced here was the *Saturday Evening Post*, a weekly magazine that often featured Norman Rockwell's pictures on the cover. Bill Pulver was an avid reader of the *Post* and looked forward to its arrival each week.

This is the cover that amused Pat.

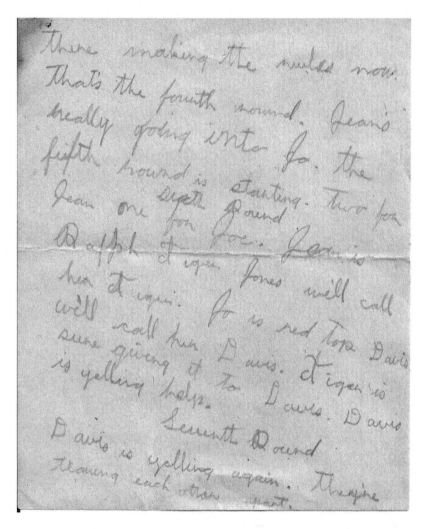

There making the rules now. That's the fourth round. Jean's really going into Jo. The fifth round is starting. Sixth Round two for Jean, one for Joe. Jean is Ralph Tiger Jones. We'll call her Tiger. Jo is red Top Davis. We'll call her Davis. Tiger is sure giving it to Davis. Davis is yelling help. Seventh Round Davis is yelling again. They're tearing each other apart.

Wrestling was popular during the '50s, and the kids were apparently fans of the sport. One wonders what Jessie must have thought of the blow-by-blow account, and perhaps she wondered why their parents had not intervened when the older sister was dominating the match to this degree. Still, all the Pulver siblings survived to adulthood.

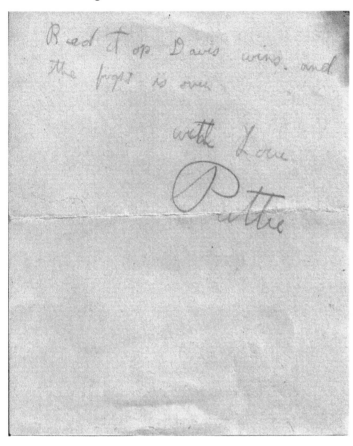

Red Top Davis wins and the fight is over.

With love, Pattie

In 1953 addresses were simpler. Jessie's grandchildren could write her name and the town and state, and the letters would be delivered with no street address or zip code. Also, the stamps were three cents then. The Pulver children continued to collect stamps, though their collections were small.

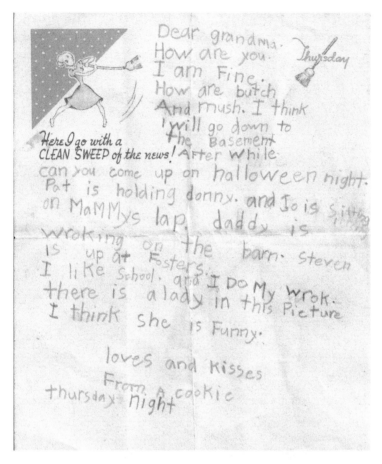

Dear Grandma, How are you. I am fine. How are Butch and Mush. I think I will go down to the basement after while. Can you come up on Halloween night. Pat is holding donny. And Jo is sitting on Mommys lap. Daddy is working on the barn. Steven is up at Fosters. I like school. And I do my work. There is a lady in this picture. I think she is Funny.

Loves and kisses

From a cookie

Thursday night

This letter was written by Jean, whose childhood nickname was Cookie.

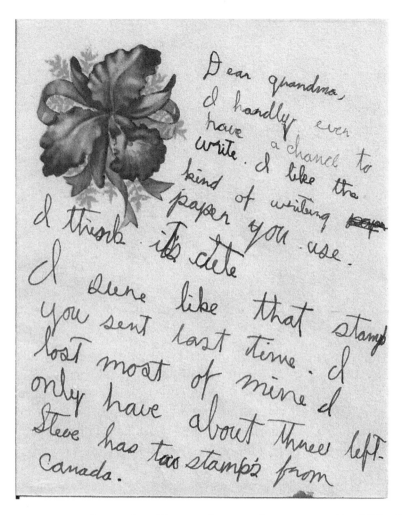

Dear Grandma, I hardly ever have a chance to write. I like the kind of writing paper you use. I think it's cute.

I sure like that stamp you sent last time. I lost most of mine. I only have about three left. Steve has two stamps from Canada.

...and Jean has one from Japan a girl at school gave it to her. I like to collect stamps. Don has a few too, but Jo doesn't.

I bet you couldn't guess what happened last night. First when we went to bed, the bull started bawling and Jean was worried, but I said he isn't out. BUT we heard mama and Daddy down stairs and they said, "The bull's out." Jean was really scared and so was Jo and the other kids. Mama finally called Herb. He came over and daddy helped him catch the bull.

With love, Pattie

A man named Herb owned a field, with cows and a bull, across Chuckanut Drive from the Pulvers. The children were in fear of the bull, and a bull in their yard, in the dark, had to be frightening.

Jan. 15, 1953

Dear Grandma,

How do you like the snow? I just went out a few minutes ago, but it's pretty cold. Thank you for the hat. I'll need it for school in this weather. It sure is cute. Tonight it's supposed to be colder. They say it's getting down to zero. I got some new cowboy boots and a pair of new shoes last Saturday.

It's sure too bad about the store. Did the sporting goods store burn too? It sure is too bad about your store.

The kids are out in the yard playing with their sleds. They can go clear from the orchard down to the driveway.

Is the snow very deep at your house?

Don got his cheeks red out in the snow. He's telling Jim Wright about the wrestling match he saw last night on TV. He says, "All they did was pull hair," even the referee was fighting.

Well I can't think of anything else to say. When you were up the other day, you know that note you left. I read it. Lots of love, Patty

P.S. Thanks again for the hat.

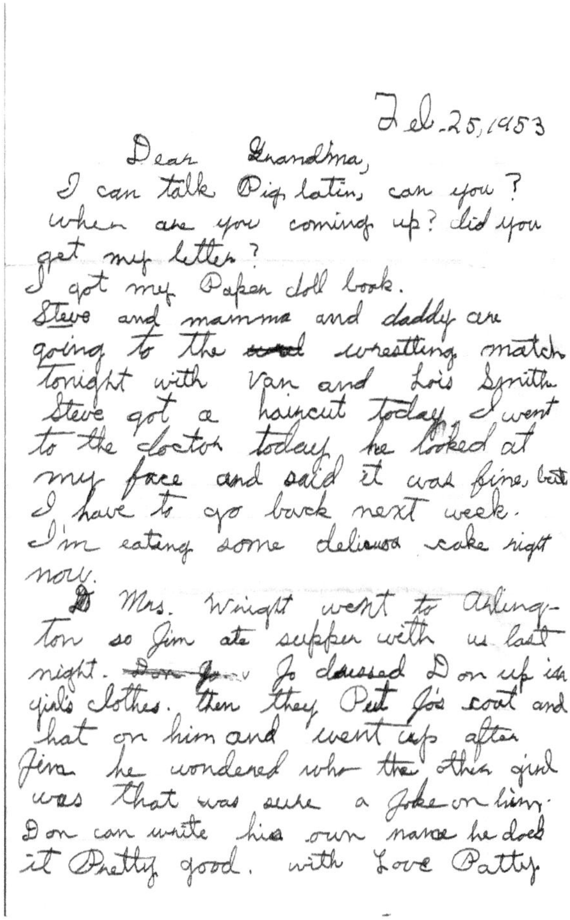

(handwritten letter reproduced below in print)

Dear Grandma,   *Feb. 25, 1953*

I can talk Pig Latin, can you? When are you coming up? Did you get my letter?

I got my paper doll book. Steve and Mamma and daddy are going to the wrestling match tonight with Van and Lois Smith. Steve got a haircut today. I went to the doctor today. He looked at my face and said it was fine, but I have to go back next week. I'm eating some delicious cake right now.

Mrs. Wright went to Arlington so Jim ate supper with us last night. Jo dressed Don up in girl's clothes, then they put Jo's coat and hat on him and went up after Jim. He wondered who the other girl was. That was sure a joke on him. Don can write his own name. He does it pretty good.

With love, Patty

By now Patty was spelling her name with a "y" at the end instead of the "ie" she had been using. Also Jo's name was now spelled simply Jo, not Joe.

Jean, Pat, Jo, and Don had dressed up in some of the old clothes at Jessie's house. Don did not look happy, and as he was four years old at this time, with three big sisters, this was probably not the last time he was dressed up as a girl.

Dear Grandma,   *Tuesday March 31, 53*

We went to a show today, it was Peter Pan. It was very good. The one that went with it was "Bear Country". It showed the bears when they were little and when they were big. I think you would like it.

I was looking in the encyclopedia, and I saw a cedar wax-wing. I couldn't find any in the encyclopedia like you were talking about.

When can you make it up to go shopping? I know what I am going to get her if I have enough money. It is a green purse, because she has green shoes and green hat and also a green scarf that she wears around her neck.

Patty was referring to Vera's birthday. She was born April 4, 1917, so she would have been thirty-six, while Patty was nine years old. Patty probably did not have enough money for a green purse at that age.

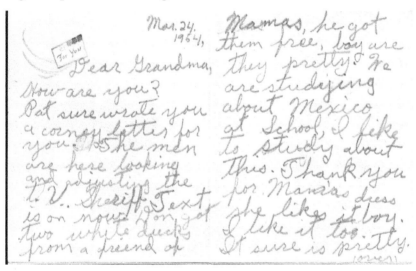

Mar. 24, 1954

Dear Grandma,

How are you? Pat sure wrote you a corney letter for you. The men are here looking and adjusting the T.V. Sheriff Text is on now. Don got two white ducks from a friend of Mamas, he got them free, boy are they pretty. We are studying about Mexico at School, I like to study about this. Thank you for Mama's dress she likes it, boy, I like it too. It sure is pretty. (Over)

This letter is from Jean who was almost ten when she wrote it. An antenna was installed on the roof, for television reception, in those days, and it was an undertaking to adjust it by turning it by hand. The Pulvers lived in a large two-story house, making it more challenging. The show she referred to was actually *Sheriff Tex* rather than Text. It was a favorite of the Pulver kids.

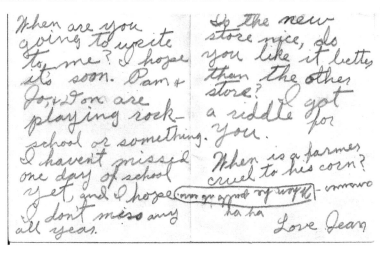

When are you going to write to me? I hope it's soon. Pam & Jo & Don are playing rock-school or something. I haven't missed one day of school yet, and I hope I don't miss any all year.

Is the new store nice, do you like it better than the other store? I got a riddle for you. When is a farmer cruel to his corn? Answer - when he pulls its ears. Ha ha

Love Jean

The dress shop where Jessie worked burned down and was relocated to Mount Vernon. The fire was referenced by Pat in a letter in 1953.

Steve, Pat, Jean, Jo, and Don Pulver

Dear Grandma, We are taking care of Eric. Don broke Eric's bottle. Joe is playing with him now.

Last night we went window shopping. We took Judy along. I am sect. of our room at school. I am a patrol too. Today was my first day – I had to go on patrol two times today. Usually I will only go on once. (This is signed "Lots of love Patty" on the back of the card.)

Eric was their neighbor and was, apparently, being watched by the Pulvers that day. Judy was most likely the daughter of a friend who was in a tuberculosis sanatorium, as Jessie had been so many years before.

May 6, 1953

Bellingham, Wash.

Dear Grandma,

What have you been doing lately? We have gotten all our ground that we want to plowed.

I am making Mamma a small clay dish for Mother's Day. I painted it blue.

Daddy shaved his beard off Sunday night.

What do you want to do Sunday? You could come up here or we might go out to Pete's for a picnic.

Bill worked forty hours a week for the telephone company, as a lineman, and after work and on weekends he maintained the five acres where they grew a large garden, a small orchard, and hay for the cattle and horses they raised.

It seems every child in elementary school made their parents presents out of clay for every holiday that required a gift. Households with children had a collection of clay bowls and ashtrays, poorly constructed but given with pride and the expectation that they would be displayed.

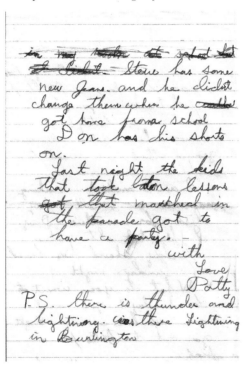

Steve has some new Jeans and he didn't change them when he got home from school. Don has his shorts on.

Last night the kids that took baton lessons that marched in the parade got to have a party.

With love Patty

P.S. There is thunder and lightning. Was there lightning in Burlington

Again, no detail was too small to report to Jessie regarding the other children in the family. The fact that Steve failed to take off his new jeans and put on his "everyday clothes" after school would have been a major transgression in the Pulver household.

Dear grandma

How are you we got 50 new baby chickens. Will you write a letter soon Vandemans were up yesterday

Love Jo

Aug. 25

Dear Grandma,

I wrote to Glenda and Loren and Grandma and Grandpa Licking. We had corn out of our garden last night. I got a bike the day before yesterday. When are you coming up? I'm getting tired.

Jean said she wanted a twin sweater set for her birthday.

Love Pat   good night

One can see, at the bottom of the letter, that Jessie answered Pat's "good night" with a whimsical "good night " of her own. Jessie's handwriting was distinctive and, to this day, is recognizable to her grandchildren.

In September of 1954, the Pulvers packed up their station wagon and drove to Nebraska for a family vacation and visit to Vera's family, who were ranchers there. The children wrote to Jessie with details of their trip.

Sat. 25, 54

Dear Grandma,

We are in _____. We got up at 2:30 this morning, now it is 7:00. We just came through Snoqualmie Pass. There was some snow sheds there. We drove through them. We saw an irrigation ditch going down a real steep hill. We are east of the mountains now. I am telling you the things I see when I see them. The trees look different here.

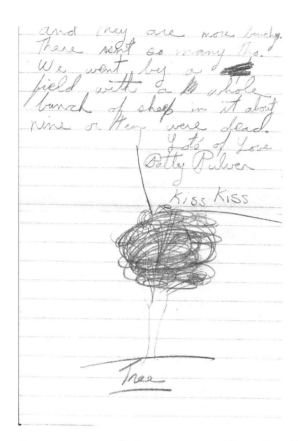

There aren't so many and they are more bunchy. There isn't so many tho. We went by a field with a whole bunch of sheep in it about nine or ten of them were dead.

Lots of love Patty Pulver

Kiss Kiss

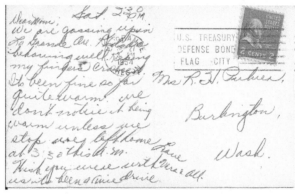

Sat. 2:30 P.M.

Dear Mom,

We are gassing up in La Grande, Ore. Kids are behaving well. Keeping my fingers crossed. It's been fine so far quite warm. We don't notice it being warm unless we stop. We left home at 3:30 this a.m. Wish you were with us. It's been a nice drive. Love, Vera & all

Vera started the trip on a positive note, with children who were behaving, but she wrote a sentence on a postcard from Jo, later in the vacation, describing the children as "wild." The close bond Jessie had with her daughter-in-law is evident in this postcard, written before they had been gone twelve hours, in which Vera says she wishes Jessie were with them. Also, Vera always called Jessie "Mom."

Dear Grandma,

We are stay at Uncle Vern's now. We went horseback riding yesterday. It was fun. I wish you were here. We sure are having fun. Mama went to see some cattle now. We saw them branding calves yesterday. It was fun watching them. Daddy helped them. We went for a ride in the jeep with Uncle Grit. It was fun. In Seneca they have real wide streets and they park in the <u>Middle</u>. Isn't that something?

The narrative of the trip to Nebraska continues in this letter.

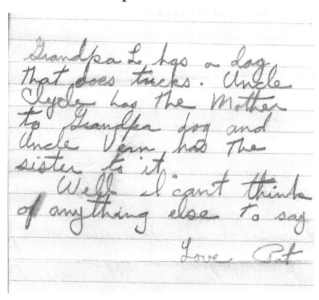

Grandpa L. has a dog that does tricks. Uncle Clyde has the Mother to Grandpa's dog and Uncle Vern has the sister to it.

Well I can't think of anything else to say.

Love, Pat

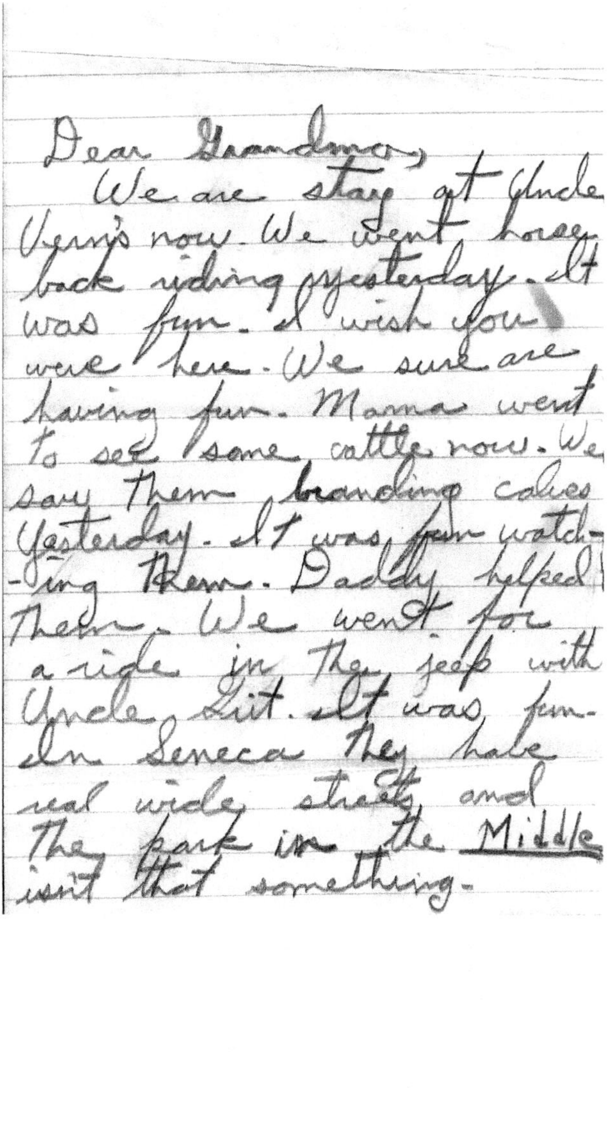

Dear Grandma,
    We are staying at Uncle
Vern's now. We went horseback riding yesterday. It
was fun. I wish you
were here. We sure are
having fun. Mama went
to see some cattle now. We
saw them branding calves
yesterday. It was fun watching them. Daddy helped
them. We went for
a ride in the jeep with
Uncle Git. It was fun.
In Seneca they have
real wide streets and
they park in the _Middle_
isn't that something.

We'll be home Fri. or Sat. everybody getting wild as all get out.

Vera wrote this note on the top of the postcard from Jo while they were in Nebraska.

Dear Grandma How are you? We will see pretty soon. Pat liked her card. I did to. We are at Grandma's now. Love Jo

Since Pat turned twelve during the trip, Jo was probably referring to a birthday card.

Sept. 30, 1954

Dear Grandma,

How are you? We are all fine. We are at Uncle Vern's and Uncle Grits. We stayed all night here. We're going out to Warren's today, we're going to go to school with them tomorrow. I stayed overnight with Dorothy Warren Tues. night. We went for a jeep ride last night and a horseback ride. They have a white pig, two dogs, a patch of watermelon and a lot of other things. I can't find anything else to say. Love, Jean

Uncle Grit and Uncle Vern were Vera's brothers, and the Warrens were Vera's sister Vada's family. Vera had seven brothers and two sisters, as well as her parents, living near Seneca, Nebraska, so there were a lot of people to see. Dorothy was a cousin close in age to Pat and Jean.

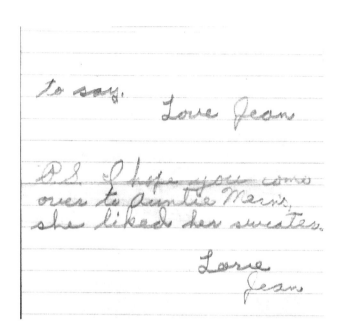

P.S. I hope you come over to Auntie Mern's, she liked her sweater.

Love, Jean

Mern was Jessie's sister-in-law, Rude's sister, and she and her husband, Harvey Sorenson, lived in Oregon. The Pulvers stopped there for a night, on their way through Oregon, on the trip to Nebraska. They planned to stay there on the way home too, and hoped that Jessie would travel to Oregon and meet them there.

Mon. a.m.

Dear Mom,

We're here in Oglalla getting a tire fixed and having lunch. We plan to keep the show on the road tonight & get to Sorenson's tomorrow night or Wed. Doesn't look like we will make much time today. It's 12 noon now. Should be home Thurs. or Fri.

We had a swell time. Everybody is fine. Must get going. Maybe we'll see you in Oregon.

Love Vera

Mern was Rude's sister and, even though Rude died in 1949, Jessie maintained a close relationship with all his siblings and their spouses throughout her life. The extended Pulver family was also close to Bill and Vera and their family.

Dear Grandma,

I love you very, very, very much.

Love Pat

Sometimes they just told Jessie they loved her.

Jean, Glenda, Jessie, Pat
Don, Jo
Loren and Steve

Chapter 7

In 1950 Margaret Jane Dunnet turned eighty-four years old. She had lived in New Brunswick, Canada all her life, but she had lived in many different towns and had traveled extensively for that time period and her income bracket. Since she was a young adult, she had written to Jessie Whitney, her sister's daughter. Jessie lived her entire life in Burlington, Washington, though she spent her last few years in Bellingham, thirty miles to the north, where her son Bill and his family lived.

Whitneyville, June 12th, 1950

Dear Jessie –

Your very interesting letter deserved an answer long ago, so did June's, but I have been a very busy person this spring. In the first place, I got busy making plans for Etta's visit, so when May 4th came, the day of her arrival in Newcastle, I had all arrangements that I could make, not having a home of my own to take her.

Jessie's sister Etta was fifty-seven years old, in 1950, when she traveled to New Brunswick to visit her mother and father's relatives. In this letter Margaret chronicles this visit.

I arranged for my nephew to meet her in Moncton, where her plane landed. The airport is over five miles from the city. He went out on May 3rd to meet her, took her to his home for the night, then next day drove her around the city, then put her on the train for Newcastle. Another nephew came with me to the depot and got her.

After supper, we went up to Sunny Corner, your Aunt Marjorie's where the son now lives.

We visited there until the 8th, then Etta came down to her Uncle Fred's and I came to Newcastle. Etta stayed a few days with Kathleen, but as K's mother is a helpless invalid, she could not entertain very well. But they took her to see some relatives in Newcastle and Chatham. Then on the 18th Etta and I went to Saint John, our oldest and largest city.

Etta paid my way. We visited Rose Tozer Mullin, your Aunt Marjorie's daughter until the 22nd, then Etta went to N.Y., Washington D.C. and other cities. She will probably be home by the time you get this letter. My Saint John friends took her all over the city. I hope she enjoyed her visit. It was very short. I wish you could come sometime but as I have no home, I cannot invite anybody.

I had to make another move. Just now I am staying with my sister-in-law, your Uncle Bob's widow. My landlady in Newcastle had to go away to Moncton to see her daughter and to help her, so the house was practically closed. It is an uncomfortable feeling to be homeless, but some day I hope to have a permanent home, where there will be no moving. So why worry!

This is an ideal time of the year to be in the country.

Margaret boarded with various people over the years or rented a room. She had mentioned earlier that her mother had left her house to her, but Margaret did not appear to live in the house at any time. It seems to have been a burden to stay with people and rent rooms, as she was so often moving or visiting for long periods of time.

...The trees along the river are beautiful. Etta would not see a more beautiful river on her journey than the Miramichi. In all my travels, I have not seen a lovelier one.

My Saint John friends think their river is very beautiful. There we saw the Reversing Falls, the only one of its kind in the world.

According to the St. John website regarding the reversing tides, "The phenomenon of the Reversing Falls is caused by the tremendous rise and fall of the tides of the Bay of Fundy, which are the highest in the world."

Margaret continued to extol the beauty of the Miramichi River, as she had in her earlier letters many years before.

The city is the oldest incorporated one in Canada founded in 1604.

Now, I must close as I have not unpacked my belongings. After a while, I plan to visit my nephew and his wife at Sunny Corner. It is a beautiful spot. Love to all your family.

Lovingly Aunt Margaret

The only other correspondence from 1950 was actually a letter to June from Margaret that she asked June to share with her mother. She apologized for not having written sooner.

I have been very unsettled. Having no permanent home keeps me moving around. I have packed and unpacked many times since June 1st. Now I am packing to go to town for the winter and longer if possible. I am tired of moving.

I had a short visit to Maine the latter part of August and the first week of September. My friend, Mrs. Emerson of Island Falls came for me and brought me back. The distance is about 200 miles. I had a trip to Bangor, a hundred miles from Island Falls. Mrs. Emerson told some friends in Newcastle that she was taking me to Maine. They told her that she must have me back before Sept. 10th as the Home and School Association, of which I am Honorary President, was putting on a party in my honor, having former pupils from the Pacific to Bermuda to write greetings to me. I wish you could see the stack of telegrams and letters which came. There was also the *presentation of a purse containing about $600. Imagine my surprise. I knew nothing about it, although plans were made during the summer... In all my long life, I have not possessed that amount of money at one time."*

In a letter to June, dated July 5, 1950, Margaret talked about the Korean War, which had begun on June 25 of that year.

The war news looks serious, doesn't it? I shudder to think of a World War III. But the show of strength in the Pacific by the USA and other nations may have a good effect, and Stalin may get the same end that Hitler and Mussolini had.

Even at age eighty-four, Margaret continued to keep up with world news. She wrote to June again in January of 1951.

The war situation does not improve. Is Truman's war policy favored in Washington? Some Republicans have voiced their approval and some decidedly not. I know Washington is a Republican state, as much as Maine. My friends in the latter state are all rank Republicans. We Canadians like President Truman. He has the courage of his convictions anyway. We like the idea of Eisenhower being in control of affairs over in Asia and Europe. It is difficult to know just how affairs are going on, as newspaper reporters are not always reliable.

Today's news might be interpreted in the same way: worry about the possibility of World War III, the news from the Mideast, and questioning the reliability of news reporters. A difference is that Washington, like Maine, is now a Democratic state rather than Republican.

Newcastle, Jan'y 14th 1951

Dear Jessie –

To-day, I feel like writing to some of my own kin. I started with June. She is such a dear, faithful correspondent, and her letters are so very interesting.

I had a nice letter from Faye at Christmas time. It looks as if she and Bill plan to live in California. I had a card from Rosamond, but did not have her address, so that I could write to her. Have you heard from Etta how she enjoyed her visit? I could do very little for her, as I had no home in which to entertain her.

Faye and Bill were Jessie's brother and sister-in-law; Rosamond and Etta were Jessie's sisters. Margaret kept in touch with all of them to varying degrees. She also wrote very regularly to Jessie's daughter, June.

Kathleen could not do much as her mother has been in bed fourteen months. She is now very frail and weak, and does not recognize anyone. But she did what she could. Wesley Tozer, your Aunt Marjorie's son had both of us visit him and his wife. I think Etta liked his wife. She is a very kind person. And we certainly enjoyed the visit to Rose in Saint John. She is quite a bit like you. I have not seen Moses Whitney, your father's cousin for a long time.

I think he is in his usual health. He will be 88 in June and looks years younger. He is very lame, and does not get around very well. I do miss your father's letters. They were always so interesting. You must miss him ever so much now that you are living in the old home. But more than that, you must miss Rude. How fine for you that June and Billy are so near!

I get terribly lonesome at times. I found a nice place for the winter with an old friend who assured me that I could stay as long as she lived, but after being there only four weeks, I had to move out.

Margaret seems particularly melancholy in this letter. It was a difficult time with the loss of so many and the uncertainty of her living situation. Jessie had lost her husband, Rude, in June of 1949, and then her father, William Hiram Whitney, in December of the same year

Her daughter, in Ontario, sent her a message saying - "If you do not come to me, I shall pack up, take my children and go back to Newcastle." Her mother knew that this meant a break-up in their marriage, so she closed her house and went. So I had to find another place. I am at the house where I stayed four or five winters before. The lady of the house is a widow, and a former pupil. But oh! I am so tired moving about. We do not have an old ladies home here. But I hope to have a permanent one someday where I will not be asked to move out.

Very soon, if I live, I shall be 85 years of age. My body is not very strong, but my memory is fairly good, and I enjoy meeting old friends. I had a wonderful Christmas with about 150 loving wishes coming to me, and wonderful gifts, some in cash, which helps ever so much. My teachers' pension is small, but I am very thankful for it. I have my burial expenses saved, a lot in the cemetery with perpetual care paid for. Hospitalization gives me five weeks in hospital free of charge. I know my Heavenly Father will care for me. With heaps of love I remain

Lovingly, Aunt Margaret

Margaret had planned well for her end of life, and she must have felt secure with five weeks of free hospitalization. She also had a strong body of support, as illustrated by the 150 Christmas greetings.

Standing in front of the Whitney house, where Jessie was living, were some of the Whitney great-grandchildren: from left - Don and Joanne Pulver, Loren Gee, Jean, Pat, and Steve Pulver, Bobby and Susan Cushen (Etta's grandchildren), and Glenda Gee.

Whitney great-grandchildren.

Newcastle, Mar. 8th, 1951

Dear Jessie -

What a good laugh I had when your birthday card of greetings came! Thank you for it and the enclosed gift. I received $13 along with many useful things. One was a mohair wool scarf from Bermuda, made in England. It is white, very fine and warm. It is much admired by many people. I received $4.00 in postage stamps.

Then along came your very interesting letter yesterday. You must have received a thought wave from me. I had been thinking of you in the old home. I can see it in my mind. How lovely for you to have Billy and June so near! I get very lonely at times. Jean and her children are in Moncton, about 100 miles from here. The baby

1 ½ years old is a darling. She has large blue eyes with long, black lashes – real Irish eyes, and the dimples are so fascinating.

At this time Jessie lived in her childhood home. It was a large Victorian style house with a few acres of fenced land. Jessie had many filbert trees with crops that she shared with family and friends.

David is 6 and does he love Aunt Margaret! He still keeps my kisses on the "back of his neck". I wish Kathleen had children. But I suppose I would spoil them.

I do enjoy June's letters. She tells me about the children. You must enjoy those lovely grandchildren. I wish I could drop down from a plane in your garden. Long ago, before flying became so popular, I used to say in your mother's letters, that I would drop down on your hen-house, some morning.

I wish you could take a trip east. I have told the cousins that they would like you ever so much.

I was interested in what you told me about Irene's keepsakes. I have the letter you wrote me about your mother's passing away. I enjoyed your father's letters ever so much.

So you had another flood. Your mother wrote me about the one that flooded their house, and drowned all the chickens, but one, and that she had to wade through two feet of water, carrying the baby. Which one, do you know?

The Skagit River, which was fairly close to the Whitney home, did flood periodically. Some of Jessie's grandchildren remember their father, Bill Pulver, going to help with sandbagging during the 1951 flood. It took the efforts of many to save the dikes which protected the property near the river.

We have had the strangest weather all this winter, and March is more like April. We have had very little snow, and when it does come, the "blower" takes it away, and soon our streets are bare. It has been very icy. I had to get "creepers" put on my overshoes. I have been alone in this 8-room apartment for nearly three weeks. My landlady is in Saint John visiting her son. She will be home on Saturday. She had the "flu" down there. I have escaped it so far. Now I must close. Do write me soon, as I am very lonely.

Kindest regards to all. Lovingly Aunt Margaret

Newcastle, Nov. 7th, 1951

Dear Jessie –

Your letter of Oct. 9th was, indeed, most welcome. But a face to face talk would be much nicer, I do wish you were nearer, so that we could meet. I can never forget how kind you were, to me, as well as to your dear mother and father. I can shut my eyes and see the old place. The orchard was most attractive. Such pears and cherries!

I am a bit stupid to-day, and sleepy. On Saturday evening, I took the bus here, and went to Fredericton, a distance of 100 miles, to be there when the Princess Elizabeth and her husband came. A friend invited me over a few days before the arrival, so that I would be rested. Well, Tuesday (yesterday) was sunny, but cold – Fredericton was in her best attire.

It is our capital city, quite old, but beautiful. The streets are laid out at right-angles, population around 10,000. It is the smallest of our N.B. cities. Its public buildings are very nice. N.B. Province presented the Princess and the Duke two beautiful motor rugs, pure wool, in air force blue, with the coat of arms of N. B. woven in them. The work was done in one of the small towns in N. B. It was on display for a few days, so I got a good look at it. The Princess is like her pictures, good-looking, and with a pleasant smile, and a wave of her hand especially to children. The Duke is really rather handsome, a blonde. He seemed to be enjoying himself as they paraded the streets escorted by a number of Royal Canadian Mounted Police, in their uniforms of scarlet coats, navy pants with yellow stripe and wide Stetson hat. Philip looks better in his naval uniform than any other apparel.

Perhaps Margaret's love of the British royalty was influenced by the fact that her ancestors had been loyal to the crown during the Revolutionary War and moved to Canada, from the US, because of their loyalty.

Little did anyone know that just two short months later Princess Elizabeth would be Queen Elizabeth and begin her lengthy reign. On February 6, 1952, while visiting Kenya, the princess learned of her father's death and her accession to the throne. Her coronation followed on June 2, 1953. In a letter to June, Margaret spoke more about the visit of Princess Elizabeth and her husband.

As the house of my friend was on Brunswick Street, on which the Princess rode in a car to the Legislative Building, I had a good view of her. Later on, I saw her on Queen St., on her way back to the railway station. Both are fine-looking, and both were smiling and waving their hands to the crowd...They lunched at the Lord Beaverbrook Hotel. It has a beautiful dining-room, one of the nicest I have seen in all my travels. It is named for one of our Newcastle boys – Lord Beaverbrook. He was here a few days ago. He has bought his old home, former manse of his father, Rev. William Aitken, Presbyterian minister.

They went to Saint John, our largest city, in the late afternoon, then on to Moncton and from there down into Nova Scotia province to Halifax.

I came home last night. Bertha Emerson, whom I visited this summer, came over from Island Falls, Maine with two young girls, to see the Princess. Bertha brought me back here, and stayed with me

*all night at my boarding-house. You know whom I mean. She was
a Whitney, your second cousin. After breakfast, she started back
to Maine. She is so very kind to me. She brought me the gift of a
lovely black, silk hat, latest style, but suitable for an old lady. It has
a black veil, which I am supposed to wear with it. It is close-fitting
and pretty flat. She sent me my summer one, also. It is very pretty
– navy blue. I wore it to her daughter's wedding in the summer.*

*What lovely note-paper you use! I use so much in my heavy cor-
respondence. I have been making my Christmas card list, and it
amounts to 109, and more to add. I get on an average five or six
letters a week from former pupils and friends. To-day, I got one
from Ottawa, from a former pupil, who has been visiting in New
York state with her husband, who also is a former pupil.*

*We have had two small snow-storms, and to-day looks stormy,
rain, I think. I put on my "woollies" to go to Fredericton, and to-
day, I have heavy foot-wear.*

*We had a reception lately for our new minister. As I had to be in
the "receiving line", I bought a dress – navy gabardine with grey
and navy over-blouse, with navy collar and cuffs – quite smart, so
my friends say. It was marked down in price – only $9.37, size 13,
so you see I am not fatter than I used to be. My hat is grey with
navy trimming to wear with it.* (back of page 1)

Margaret Jane Dunnet

I am saving on note-paper. My pen is like my tongue, it goes on and on.

I was up in Whitneyville since I wrote to you, called to see Kathleen, Ernest, Nelson and family, also your Aunt Ruth, brother Bob's widow. The old home seems so empty to me - I am the only one of the family left. I feel lonely at times. There is no one to whom I can say "Do you remember?" The young ones would not know who I am talking about. It is so nice that you can see June and Billy occasionally. I saw my niece, Jean, in Moncton in September. She has two lovely children, David and Marjorie Ruth. Of all the "grands" I love David best. He is 6 past - goes to school now. Ruthie is two, has lovely blue eyes with long lashes, and charming dimples. I missed seeing Margaret, Jean's sister. She lives in Montreal.

When Margaret wrote these words about loving her nephew David the most, she could not have known that the others might see her words in this book someday. They might agree that a great-aunt at eighty-plus years of age is probably entitled to a favorite though.

Jessie with June and Bill about this time.

She has one child – a boy. I think I told you about him. When he was here on a visit with his mother, he did not become very friend- ly with his "nanna". He would say "other nanna", meaning me. He would follow me everywhere. Nelson's children are much older. The boy thirteen and the girl eleven. The latter is taking music down here, and is getting on well. Her teacher has her, with other pupils to sing or play over the radio.

I think I mentioned my nice boarding house. Am very happy. On Jan. 1st, all people over 70 will get $40 a month pension, so I will be on "easy street" along with my teacher's pension. The latter does not pay my board. Sometimes it was hard going. But my heavenly Father has cared for me in a wonderful way through kind friends.

I had a letter from the cousin Jenny (Macaulay) Easson who flew from Scotland to the Pacific Coast, and who now lives in Vancou- ver. Her mother was Margaret Dunnet. Jenny's grandfather, and your mother were first cousins - Etta called to see her not long ago, along with Ella Ingram, who used to visit your mother when I was there. Two other relatives of yours live in Vancouver. Gordon Whitney and his wife. Both are related, on the Whitney side. Wish you could meet them. Why not come to see us next year?

Well, this is some letter. I must stop at once. You will be tired out. Love to your own dear ones and yourself.

Lovingly, Aunt Margaret

p.s. You spoke of my writing. Yours is beautiful. Aunt M.

Newcastle, Dec. 8th, 1951

Dear Jessie,

As a rule, I do not send my "thank you" letters until after Christmas. I was so delighted to get your very welcome gift to-day. Yes, I surely can use them. So far, I have bought about four dollars worth. Our postal rates on parcels and unsealed Christmas cards have gone up. Where we only put one cent on a card, with envelope tucked in, now we pay two - I send out over a hundred cards, many of them having four cents on them. Visiting around so much adds more friends to be remembered.

During Margaret's lifetime, postage rates increased infrequently, and there was the option of sending a letter third class, at a lower rate, which meant the flap of the envelope was tucked in rather than sealed. That was also an option in the US until 1968. Many people chose to send their Christmas cards this way to save money.

The cost of the first ounce of mail from Canada to the US was stable, at two cents, from 1899 until 1915. From 1915 to 1926 a war tax was added, making the cost three cents (two cents for the first ounce and an additional one cent, on the first ounce only, for the war tax). This price remained in effect until 1926, when the war tax was removed and the cost went back to two cents. In 1931 the war tax was reinstated, and it lasted until 1951, when it was again removed. The war tax was only one cent until 1943, when it became two cents. In 1951 the war tax was incorporated into the cost of a stamp, making the letter rate four cents.

In 1951, the cost was increased to five cents, which meant that the cost of a stamp increased three cents during most of Margaret's lifetime. One wonders what she would have thought about the increase in Canada, in 2014, from sixty-three cents to eighty-five cents for a first class letter, a 35 percent increase.

Do you remember giving me, on one of my visits, a snapshot album with some lovely Burlington views? There are some lovely scenes among the pictures - Chuckanut Drive, for instance. Now, when I pass on to my Heavenly home, there is no one who would be interested here. None of them ever had the pleasure of meeting you or your family. So I am planning to mail the album to you. Will send it in care of Bill Forsyth's nephew, Gordon Whitney or to Mrs. Will Ingram. Then you will have no duty. Bill can bring it back to you sometime when he goes up to B.C.

Margaret always liked to send packages across Canada when she could to save duty. She also mentioned mailing things when she was in Maine to save the duty that would otherwise need to be paid.

But how nice if you could go to Vancouver! Gordon Whitney and wife are related to you on both sides, Bertie's grandmother and your mother were first cousins: Gordon's father and yours were first cousins. The Scottish cousin - Mrs. John Easson, who flew from Scotland to B.C., is also related to you. Her mother was Margaret Dunnet, a cousin of your mother. Another relative in Vancouver is a Mrs. Condo, whose grandmother and your mother were first cousins.

Don't tell the other members of the family about the album. You have the best right to it. Etta asked for it. Thanking you, I remain, Yours lovingly, Aunt Margaret

Margaret seemed to increasingly feel the need to tell Jessie about her extended family so that there might be communication between them and the ties between the New Brunswick and Washington branches of the family would not be lost. She would probably be pleasantly surprised to find that many years later, in 2014, Jessie's granddaughter, Patricia Pulver Fitzgerald, and Ruth Somers, Margaret's brother Robert's granddaughter, would connect via social media to share pictures and information.

Ruth is the baby referred to as Jean's daughter and David's little sister in Margaret's letters.

Newcastle, January 1st, 1952.

Dear Jessie –

This is my second letter this year. The other one was to a Scotch cousin who came to live in Vancouver last year. She is the one who flew from Scotland, and I met her in Montreal, on her way west. As she is far from her home, she likes to get letters. Her mother was Margaret Dunnet. She calls me "Aunt Margaret." Her youngest brother is in Africa so the family is widely separated. He sent me a card for Christmas, by air. It cost 2 shillings to send it. I can send him an air letter for 15 cts.

Hope you had a nice Christmas season. You surely would with all those charming grandchildren.

I had a letter from Bill and Vera in their Christmas card.

I received 176 cards, all with lovely messages, and from far separated countries. There were several from Scotland, one from Bermuda, one from East Africa (as I mentioned) and numbers from the Pacific Coast. I received some lovely gifts to the number of 51. I have sent or said "thank you" to all but one. Yours was the first. Besides yours, I received $4 worth of postage stamps and about $70 in cash. One cheque was for $25 from our Senator. He is a former pupil and sent me the same last year. Friends were more than kind. I have enough note paper to last me a year, or more. I received 3 pairs of stockings a "nightie", a nylon slip, two scarfs, an apron some "hankies", a book, three calendars, two of which came from Scotland with lovely views, two Magazine subscriptions, hand lotion, 2 boxes of chocolates, and a pound of peppermints, this small note paper is from Bill Dunnet, whose mother was born in Scotland. It is at his home I visit in Bangor.

To-day there was a funeral in Whitneyville. Hiram Whitney, a cousin of your fathers died Sunday morning after a long illness. His son, Gordon lives in Vancouver. Etta has met them. Bill Forsyth and wife have been there to see them. Gordon took a plane Sunday night, and was here Monday night. He will be back in

Vancouver to-morrow

Love to all your family. Lovingly - Aunt Margaret

P.S. I spent Christmas day in Whitneyville - Had a pleasant time.

Again, Margaret discussed the cost of postage. However, with her extensive letter writing, it must have been a significant expenditure with her limited resources.

Newcastle, Feb. 24th, 1952

Dear Jessie -

Many thanks for your nice Valentine and enclosed note. It arrived when I was visiting in Moncton and was sent on. I received such a pleasant surprise when a Valentine came from Mrs. Simons, a little note and a pretty handkerchief with little red hearts all over it. She told me of visiting you. I received valentines from Glenda and Loren, Faye and Bill and June.

Moncton is a nice city. It was to the Moncton Airport that Etta landed, nearly two years ago. My nephew, who lives there, met her and kept her at his home until next day, when he put her on the train for Newcastle.

I stayed there two weeks with some old friends who formerly lived here - Mr. and Mrs. Hayward. Mr. H. is President of a Company with chain stores over a large part of New Brunswick. I have known him since he was 18. Now he is about 75. His wife is a bit younger, also a native of Newcastle. They have a lovely modern home. I was in danger of being spoiled, having breakfast in bed - etc. Food? They started in with a 15 lb. Turkey!! That was a treat, as I only taste it once a year. But I really like plain food. As soon as I get my camera films printed, I must send you one of the snow-drifts here. It has been one of the worst Februarys in 50 years, as far as I know.

It snowed every day last week except on Saturday, with high winds which blocked traffic. But our Canadian National Railways coped with the snow-drifts in a wonderful way. I came home on Friday, and the heavy train- all Pullmans arrived on time. One has to have a special ticket to travel on this train, so Mr. Hayward took my "coach" ticket to the depot and bought a "standard" in place, paying a little extra. We have had numerous accidents since the storms started. Big overseas planes had to come to the Moncton Airport, as they could not land any other place. This morning, a bus, loaded with early church-goers - Roman Catholic skidded into two places of business in Campbellton.

Margaret mentioned that it had snowed six days the previous week, which must have been quite unusual as, historically, there have usually been just ten days of precipitation in February, according to the website WhatstheWeatherLike.org.

We have not yet heard how many were injured.

I think I have told you that we have our own broad-casting station. Local people are often mentioned. Your Uncle Ed was very much pleased when he and your Aunt May received congratulations on their golden wedding anniversary. I usually get birthday congratulations, so everybody knows how old I am. It is no secret around the Miramichi. I had a nice letter from Charlotte Forsyth, in answer to a Christmas card I sent. I did not go to church this morning, as I do not hear well. But I can hear over the radio, so this morning our own minister where I board was on the air. The church is quite near.

The Uncle Ed and Aunt May referred to here are Margaret's younger brother, Edward, and his wife.

The Scottish cousins keep up a correspondence with me. There are five or six. One moved to Vancouver, and I hear from her. I think Etta has met her, also Mrs. Ingram. Her mother was Margaret Dunnet. I think I told you of meeting her in Montreal when she flew there from Scotland. Your mother and her grandfather were first cousins. Just in case you should go to Vancouver sometime, I shall give you her *address. She writes that she and her husband may go to Seattle for a trip sometime. I wish I could have gone to Scotland.*

My niece, Marguerite, your Uncle Bob's daughter, when she was overseas as an army nurse, visited all these cousins. Were they delighted! One of them sends her heather every year.

Yes, we sincerely mourn the death of our beloved king. Having seen him and his wife in 1929, when they visited Newcastle, made him seem more real. I took their pictures at that time, as I was an official guest at their reception. Now, I am glad that I went to Fredericton to see Princess Elizabeth, our present queen. She is young to have so much responsibility, but she was trained for it.

On Friday, the 15th, it was a real day of mourning. All places of business, and schools were closed; flags at half mast, and services were held in the different churches. I was in Moncton then. It was strange to hear the people sing "God Save the Queen". I am enclosing one card from the daily paper. Instead of business "ads", the space was filled by testimonials to a beloved ruler.

I have written a note to Mrs. Simons; now I must write to June. Loren received a birthday card from David (also 7) and is going to write to him. David is my niece's boy and I dearly love him. Jean has a little daughter, pretty as a picture. I had supper with them when in Moncton.

Heaps of love, Aunt Margaret

Margaret spoke again of her affection for David. In an earlier letter to June, when speaking of David, she stated, "If I had not neglected an important duty when I was young I might have had some great-grands, too." Margaret was eighty-six when she wrote this letter.

Newcastle, Mar. 8th, 1952

Dear Jessie –

Many thanks for your birthday card of kind wishes and enclosed gift. I had a wonderful celebration. Was invited out to supper. There was a birthday cake with candles (not 86 however) and a delicious supper with a gift beside my plate.

I received $16, $5.50 worth of postage stamps a dozen carnations, two boxes of chocolates, hankies and other gifts and about fifty cards. A telegram came from my niece in Toronto, and birthday wishes over the radio. We have our own broadcasting station here.

My oldest friend in Newcastle died on my birthday. When I came to teach in Newcastle in 1891, I boarded with her. It was at her home that your mother and father had supper the evening they were married. I took Etta in to see them when she was east. I also took her to the Parsonage where they were married by a Methodist minister, Dr. John Clark.

I had birthday cards from Etta, Faye & Bill and June.

I think our snowstorms are over. There are still piles of snow...

...in the country. Our town has the reputation of keeping very clean streets but when all this snow melts, we shall have some wading to do. Please excuse this short letter. I have a great many "thank yous" to write. Love to Bill and family, and to your dear self.

Lovingly, Aunt Margaret

Newcastle, May 17th, 1953

Dear Jessie –

Your lovely "Mother's Day" card and enclosed pictures pleased me very much. What a good-looking group of children! I was surprised to see Glenda so tall. She must be as tall, if not taller, than her mother. I would love to see you all. What a pleasant time you must have had together!

Lately, I have had a nervous upset, and the medicine the doctor prescribed has made me rather stupid. I must stop it. My memory is poor, in consequence. So this letter will be short. I had a very nice one from June shortly before yours. Have not heard from Etta for over two months. I think Charlotte owes me a letter.

This photo of Jessie and her grandchildren was taken in the living room at Jessie's house. They are, in the chair, from left to right: Loren and Steve, and standing: Jean, Glenda, Jessie, Don, Pat, and Joanne.

I received two magazines lately from Ella Ingram in Vancouver. In them was a write-up on Lord Beaverbrook - much of it far from the truth.

We have a holiday to-morrow three-in-one. It is really Loyalist Day, but three, "Victoria Day" Queen Elizabeth's birthday, and Loyalist. The second of June will be Coronation Day, and July 1st Dominion Day. The holidays are coming in a bunch. We are to have a big celebration on June 2nd. Hope to get some snaps.

Would you mind sending me Rosamond's address? Would like to write to her.

I received some lovely roses on Mother's Day and a dainty Coro-

nation brooch. My new dress is navy and white, my hat all navy, also "shortie coat". My favorite colors.

Love to all the family. Did Loren get the coin?

Lovingly, Aunt Margaret

Lord Beaverbrook, born a Canadian named Maxwell Aitken, made a fortune, moved to England, and became involved in politics. He served in British cabinet positions in both world wars and then became a philanthropist who was very generous to New Brunswick. The Beaverbrook Foundation website states the following:

After the War, Lord Beaverbrook served as Chancellor of the University of New Brunswick and became the university's greatest benefactor, fulfilling the same role for the city of Fredericton and the Province as a whole. He provided additions to the University, scholarship funds, the Beaverbrook Art Gallery, the Beaverbrook Skating Rink, the Lord Beaverbrook Hotel, the Playhouse, and many other projects. He once estimated that he had given some $16 million to various causes in New Brunswick alone. He set up and chaired Foundations both in the UK and Canada to further his philanthropic aims. Lord Rosbery said of him: "He used his wealth unostentatiously, sometimes not even letting his right hand know what his left hand did. He helped many in distress. I have known even his enemies, of whom he had many, to be helped by him anonymously when he heard that they were in an impoverished condition."

179 City Road, Saint John, N.B.

July 26th, 1953

Dear Jessie –

Our last letters crossed on the way. Mine was an air letter. I sent it from Island Falls Maine, also one to Etta by the same mail. When Faye wrote me in the spring about their planning to come, she asked me not to mention it as something might happen to prevent, so I did not tell you people until they were actually here. We all enjoyed their visit.

On my way back from Island Falls, when I left, June 30th, I went to Fredericton where I visited until July 6th, then came here to visit my niece, Rose (Tozer) Mullin

Faye was Jessie's sister-in-law, her brother Bill's wife.

I think I told you in my letter that Bill and Faye stayed here all night on our way to Island Falls, Maine. It is an interesting old city, the oldest incorporated city in Canada. I am planning to leave here on Tuesday, 28th. The weather is usually cool here. Up home, in Newcastle, they have had some nineties, 94 and 95 (degrees). I am glad I escaped it.

Bill and Faye arrived home on the 30th of June, travelling the 10,000 miles in six weeks, minus 2 days. They must have been very tired. Bill had a good car – Lincoln - and is a good driver. Had a letter from Etta a few days ago. She said that she called to see you when the Scottish cousin, Jenny Easson, her husband and father had come from Vancouver to spend a week-end with her.

and father had come from Vancouver to spend a week-end with her. Jenny will probably write me. Her father flew from Scotland, was given a pass over the C.P.R. from the Montreal Airport. He is a retired railway man. I went to Montreal to meet Jenny when she flew to Canada five years ago. Her mother was Margaret Dunnet, the daughter of my first cousin, so you can figure out your relationship. I was the first relative to greet her in Canada. When you come, (by air?) a first cousin will meet you in Moncton. But a trip across Canada by train is more interesting. The scenery is really beautiful

Jenny will probably write me. Her father flew from Scotland, was given a pass over the C.P.R. (Canadian Pacific Railway) from the Montreal Airport. He is a retired railway man. I went to Montreal to meet Jenny when she flew to Canada five years ago. Her mother was Margaret Dunnet, the daughter of my first cousin, so you can figure out your relationship. I was the first relative to greet her in Canada. When you come, (by air?) a first cousin will meet you in Moncton. But a trip across Canada by train is more interesting. The scenery is really beautiful.

Jessie never went to New Brunswick, but this letter implies that she was planning to and that it was not just Margaret's wishful thinking. Margaret continued to describe what Jessie would see on this trip.

You will see "Mount Eisenhower" which was re-named for your President. It was formerly Castle Mountain. You see how much we admire your President although he was not then a candidate.

I had a nice letter from June when she was packing for her new home.

I was dreaming of Burlington this morning, having awakened early, then went to sleep and had the dream.

You will love Rose and family. She is, in many ways, like your mother. Bill and Faye noticed that. She is your Aunt Marjorie's eldest daughter.

> with Kathleen, than with the
> other cousins. Bill liked
> being in his mothers old home,
> and he and K's husband took
> a fancy to each other. K.
> gave him his grandmother's old
> spinning-wheel. He seemed
> to loved antiques.
> I showed him the old cemetery
> three miles out of Newcastle.
> where your great, great, great
> grandfather and grandmother
> are buried. He took a picture
> of their gravestone, also of one
> of his Whitney ancestors, also
> a great-great-great.
> Some friends of mine gave them
> a lonely trip down the river

Bill and Faye spent more time with Kathleen, than with the other cousins. Bill liked being in his mother's old home, and he and K's husband took a fancy to each other. K. gave him his grandmother's old spinning-wheel. He seemed to love antiques.

I showed him the old cemetery three miles out of Newcastle where your great, great, great-grandfather and grandmother are buried. He took a picture of their gravestone, also of one of his Whitney ancestors, also a "great-great-great".

Some friends of mine gave them a lovely trip down the river over 50 miles.

We had dinner at an Inn. We were given freshly-caught salmon. Miramichi salmon are considered the finest in N.B. They were much interested in the Indian names here - quite different from those on the Pacific Coast. Miramichi means "Happy Retreat", Restigouche - "five fingered river "Quispamsis "little lake" and so on.

At this time, Wikipedia translates Quispamsis as "little lake in the woods."

Rose hopes you can come. She is prepared to <u>love</u> you as I have talked so much about you. All the cousins have cars, so they can take you around.

I may not have very much longer as I am now 87 + some months.

I had a card from Ella Ingram, written from California where she is keeping house for her sister who went over to the coronation. What a big event that was! Hope we will get some prettier stamps. This is poor, and she is really good-looking. I had a close view of her when she visited New Brunswick.

Heaps of love – Address Newcastle

Lovingly, Aunt Margaret

Love to Billy's family.

Sideways in the margin, Margaret had written, "This is really badly written. Hand shaky."

Margaret, at eighty-seven years old, showed strong handwriting and a clear mind. She was able to write a seven-page letter about a variety of topics, even the English meaning of the Native Canadians' names for local places. She remained loyal to the British royalty and current in her information about them.

Newcastle, Sept. 27th, 1953

Dear Jessie –

In looking over one of your letters, I found a paragraph, which I must have missed or forgot. I have a habit of re-reading your lovely letters.

You asked about the genealogy of your mother's family. As I looked up a little for Bill, I think I can remember some, if not all. It is not a regular family tree, just some events. Do you remember "Aunty Rogers"? She was Ann Forsyth, a sister of your grandmother Dunnet. There were no "Annies" in those days. She was always called "Ann" by the family.

The enclosed card shows a bit of country where the Dunnets lived. There is a village called Dunnet.

When your mother was born, Aunty R. was working in Mass. where many Canadian girls went to work in mills, weaving. So she called herself "Annie". She wished your mother to be named "Annie Rose" or just "Rose" as there was another Annie Dunnet. She was never called "<u>Anna</u>". The family Bible has it "Annie Rose". Well, that does not matter, except that Etta said to me that her name <u>was</u> "<u>Anna</u>". Grandfather Dunnet and his wife Ann Nicholson D. came to this country in 1823, bringing a baby girl a few months old. They came in a sailing vessel.

Margaret was making it clear, in this letter, that her sister

was named Annie, not Anna, though as an adult she was called
Anna or Rose.

Ann Forsyth would have been thirty-two years old when
she worked in the mills and her niece, Anna Rose Dunnet, was
born. Five years later, Ann Forsyth would be Annie Rogers and
would have a daughter of her own whom she would also name
Anna.

*What hardships they suffered! They raised a large family – four
girls and five boys. One of the boys was Edward, your grandfather.
Your grandmother was Jane Forsyth, daughter of Robert Forsyth Jr.
who was a son of Robert Forsyth, Senior who fought in the Revolutionary War on the side of the British. The Forsyths go back a long*

way in history, when there were titles in the family. Robert Forsyth Senior married Jane Martin, daughter of William and Mary Ann Martin whose graves are in the old Cemetery here, about 3 miles from Newcastle. We took Bill to see the place.

In this account of the family, Margaret does not mention that when her grandparents left Scotland, in 1823, they left their two-year-old son behind with his grandfather. Missing their son must have been part of the hardships they suffered.

These were the graves of his and your great-great-great grand-parents. Ebenezer Whitney's grave is also there. He is a great-great-great-grandfather also. Bill took pictures of their grave-stones.

Your grandmother's mother was Margaret Mackinnon daughter of Gregor Mackinnon who also fought in the Revolutionary War. He married a so called "rebel" Jane Pierson. She was disowned by her family. One of the Mackinnon girls lived to be 104. Both Mackinnons and Forsyths received grants of land on this river. Now, can you build a family tree? By the way, Forsyth has no "e" at the end of the name as Bill uses. When I write them I do not use it.

The Dunnets came from the
north of Scotland - Caithness.
You can find the name
"Dunnet" on the map.
I cannot find out anything
farther back than my
grandfather. The scottish
people laugh about genealogy.
It may not be safe for
some of them, as they might
have an ancestor hanged
for sheep-stealing ha ha.
When you come to see us,
I shall try to show you
the old cemetery. Lord
Beaverbrook has restored it
and enclosed it. It is now
called "The Enclosure." There
is an "Annie Forsyth" buried
there. I fancy she was grand-
fathers sister. I wish I knew
more. Your Grandfather (great)

(margin:) If you are a bit clannish, you can wear the Sinclair tartan, also Mackinnon and

In the margin, Margaret wrote, "If you are a bit clannish, you can wear the Sinclair tartan, also Mackinnon and Cameron and Nicolson."

The Dunnets came from the north of Scotland – Caithness. You can find the name "Dunnet" on the map. I cannot find out anything farther back than my grandfather. The Scottish people laugh about genealogy. It may not be safe for some of them, as they might have an ancestor hanged for sheep-stealing <u>ha</u> <u>ha.</u>

When you come to see us, I shall try to show you the old cemetery. Lord Beaverbrook has restored it and enclosed it. It is now called "The Enclosure". There is an "Annie Forsyth" buried there. I fancy she was grandfather's sister. I wish I knew more.

As she reached the end of her life, Margaret seemed eager to pass on family history. One wonders what she would think of the online resources available today, where it is possible to uncover one's ancestors with a few clicks of a mouse.

Jessie's great-great-grandfather, Robert Forsyth Sr., was born in 1783, in Pennsylvania, and went to New Brunswick, Canada with others who had been loyal to Britain during the Revolutionary War. He married Jane Martin after abducting her from her family, according to court records. Jessie's great-grandfather, Robert Forsyth Jr., was born in New Brunswick in 1804. He was the one whose sword Margaret had and then passed on to a grandnephew.

was a Captain who drilled men during a ten-day period. I had his sword, but gave it to my grand-nephew. The drilling was called "The Muster". He was better educated than the neighbors, and was appointed a magistrate. Very few of the settlers were educated even to a small degree. He was a very fine writer. Perhaps that is where you get your fine hand. Your Grandfather Whitney was secretary of school trustees when I taught in Whitneyville a very fine person. Bill met one first cousin on the Whitney side, but quite a number on the Dunnet side.

Your grandfather (great) was a captain who drilled men during a ten-day period. I had his sword, but gave it to my grand-nephew. The drilling was called "The Muster". He was better educated than the neighbors, and was appointed a magistrate. Very few of the settlers were educated even to a small degree. He was a very fine writer. Perhaps that is where you get your fine hand. Your Grandfather Whitney was secretary of school trustees when I taught in Whitneyville a very fine person. Bill met one first cousin on the Whitney side, but quite a number on the Dunnet side.

Your Uncle Fred's family are scattered – only Harold left here.

A cousin gave a party for Bill and Faye and invited all the "clan". Your Uncle Fred's widow was there. I was too tired to go as I acted as guide on their visits to other cousins, and could not take in evening affairs. But I enjoyed them all. All the cousins "fell" for Bill, and they liked Faye. Bill enjoyed his mother's old home more than the others quite naturally.

Kathleen, my niece, who lives in the old home, gave Bill his grandmother's spinning wheel. He got another one somewhere. I must close. Have been out for a long ride, and am sleepy.

Heaps of love - Aunt Margaret

Newcastle, Mar. 22nd, 1954

Dear Jessie -

It seems to me that I owe you a letter. I have written over a hundred letters since Jan. 1st. Hope yours was one of them, and June, also. What a faithful correspondent she is! I know she wrote me inside of a birthday card. Hope you are well. You will be having green grass and leaves coming out, no doubt.

On Saturday, we had one of our wildest snow-storms. Now it is melting and what a slop!

As my eyes have been giving me some trouble, I went to Moncton, nearly a hundred miles from here, by train, last Thursday afternoon, to consult an oculist. He happens to be an old pupil of mine, and quite famous in his line. I had no appointment, so when I went to his office on Friday morning, his secretary said, No, you cannot see him until after Easter!!

until after E²aster !! There were
about half-a-dozen people waiting,
all having appointments. I said
that I would like to speak to Dr.
Desmond for about two minutes,
and gave her my name. She
returned and said Dr. Desmond
will see you. Much to my surprise,
and gratitude, he took me at once
and examined my eyes. Was I lucky!
He gave me a prescription and we
had a few minutes chat. He was a
lovely boy in school. Afterwards,
when he enlisted as a medical
officer. War II he wrote me from France
and other places where he was
stationed. His father was a doctor
in Newcastle, a friend of mother's.
I had no bill to pay. I stayed
all night with my niece, Jean,
and her family, and returned
home Friday afternoon, being in
Moncton less than 24 hours. I also
made a call on a sick friend

There were about half a dozen people waiting, all having appointments. I said that I would like to speak to Dr. Desmond for about two minutes, and gave her my name. She returned and said Dr. Desmond will see you. Much to my surprise, and gratitude, he took me at once and examined my eyes. Was I lucky! He gave me a prescription and we had a few minutes chat. He was a lovely boy in school. Afterwards, when he enlisted as a medical officer in World War II, he wrote me from France and other places where he *was stationed. His father was a doctor in Newcastle, a friend of mother's. I <u>had</u> <u>no</u> <u>bill</u> <u>to</u> <u>pay</u>.*

I stayed all night with my niece, Jean, and her family and returned home Friday afternoon, being in Moncton less than 24 hours. I also made a call on a sick friend.

Margaret had continued relationships with many of her former students. At this time, Margaret would have been eighty-eight years old so it had been many years since she had taught the students she wrote about. They must have been very fond of her as she cites many examples of generous gifts from them, including this free eye exam.

swift work? for an old dame of 88 years. Surely I have been wonderfully cared for by my many friends. Have I written you about my birthday celebration? It was a big one - Received over fifty messages from many places. The last one was an air message from the north of Scotland. The Home and School Association sent me roses (I am their Honorary President) A friend, a former pupil invited me to supper. She had a beautifully decorated cake with candles. Daffodils, tulips and carnations also were sent by friends. Bertha (Whitney) Emerson, being in Maine, sent daffodils. (my flower) Bill and Faye visited her on their way home last summer. Are you coming east this year? We will give you a hearty welcome. Etta wrote me that she plans to go to California early in April. How nice for her! Love to your dear ones in Bellingham, and to your dear self. Lovingly, Aunt Margaret

Swift work for an old dame of 88 years. Surely I have been wonderfully cared for by my many friends. Have I written you about my birthday celebration? It was a big one – Received over fifty messages from many places. The last one was an air message from the north of Scotland.

The Home and School Association sent me roses (I am their Honorary President). A friend, a former pupil, invited me to supper. She had a beautifully decorated cake with candles. Daffodils, tulips and carnations also were sent by friends Bertha (Whitney) Emerson, living in Maine, sent daffodils. (my flower) Bill and Faye visited her on their way home last summer.

Are you coming east this year? We will give you a hearty welcome. Etta wrote me that she plans to go to California early in April. How nice for her!

Love to all your dear ones in Bellingham, and to your dear self.

Lovingly, Aunt Margaret

Newcastle, Mar. 6th, 1955

Dear Jessie –

Many thanks for greetings and gift, also your letter. All were appreciated. I had a most enjoyable celebration on my 89th birthday. What changes I have seen during the long years! Also many pleasures and many woes. I have crossed the continent from the Atlantic to the Pacific six times going and returning; have had two plane flights (not very long) have lived through <u>four</u> wars; was born at the close of the American Civil War (cannot remember it) I visited the USA during the Spanish American War, and now the Korean trouble. Hope it will soon be cleared up.

Of course, Margaret had also lived through the two world wars.

An old pupil of mine is arriving to-day from Bellingham, Wash. to visit her sister who is sick. I hope to see her.

I received over 50 greeting cards from places between the Atlantic and Bermuda and Pacific - Many lovely flowers came. The "Home and School Association" of which I am Honorary President sent some lovely daffodils (my particular flower), friends, now in Florida, left an order in the nursery for daffodils, mums and tulips. A friend in Maine always sends American Beauty roses, but this year they did not come. She may be sick, had three birthday cakes, three or four boxes of chocolates; a lovely nightie, several hdkfs (handkerchiefs), bath towel and face cloths. Don't let anyone see this writing. I do not like the parchment variety.

I attended church this morning for the first time in three months. I am feeling stronger. Got a ride home, however. The streets are very icy. We have heaps of snow. Bill Forsyth's sister has been in Regina, and I was told that she rang him up. I had a card from Bill and Charlotte for my birthday. Bill has a nephew in Regina with the Ford Motor Company. I had greetings from June, Glenda, and Loren. What good writers the children are! I suppose Bill W. is very proud of being a grandfather. I must stop this scribbling. Heaps of love to you and family.

Lovingly, Aunt Margaret

Bill and Charlotte Forsyth lived in Seattle and were frequent visitors of the Pulvers in Bellingham. Bill Pulver and Bill Forsyth referred to themselves as forty-second cousins, but they were not that far removed.

Newcastle, Aug. 18th, 1955

Dear Jessie –

Do not get a shock at receiving a reply so promptly. I owed you a letter before yours came, anyway, also June. I have written to her yesterday, so now my conscience is not troubling me so much.

We had such a hot, dry summer, that I felt wilted, and not in a letter-writing mood. Yesterday and to-day are cool and cloudy, and I have to wear a sweater. It will not be long until all the days are cool.

It is predicted that the winter is to be very cold and stormy. Hope not. I have just received a call from my nephew who lives in Moncton. He is the one who met Etta at the airport when she came east. He is your first cousin; has four children - two boys and two girls. Bill Forsyth went to see him when he landed. He has two barber shops in the city; a nice home and car.

I have not heard from Etta for quite a long time. Have written to her lately.

written to her lately.

I have not been very well lately. What do I expect? I think you are working too hard. Why not live a life of leisure? You do not need to work, do you? Your garden would give you enough to do. Now, perhaps this sounds like <u>impudence</u>, but what I learned from Etta, I thought Rude left you well-to-do, that the property was valuable, and in addition your father's property. Please do not say I told you this. It is really none of my business. Everything is so high now-a-days.

Perhaps because Margaret so often spoke of her own financial situation, she did not feel out of line discussing Jessie's, although she did say it might sound impudent.

But do take care of yourself.

What a comfort to you to have June, Bill and family! I feel so alone. I have many nieces and nephews but they are all wrapped up in their families. My niece in Saint John is very kind, and so is Kathleen, your Uncle Ed's daughter, but there is a certain amount of jealousy as her father left her the homestead. She cared well for her mother and father, and the others did not, so she deserved it. She is not very well just now. The doctor said she had a heart condition and must rest. Yes we would love to have you. I have told them that they would be sure to like you. Love to your own folks and regards to my acquaintances. Sincerely, Aunt Margaret

As she got older and was less mobile, Margaret sometimes spoke about being lonely even though she seemed to have a large number of friends and kept in touch with so many of her former students. In a letter to June, at this time, she wrote about receiving a plant from one of her former pupils, now a senator in Ottawa, who sent her "a lovely cyclamen, red blossom. It is still blooming. He has been sending me gifts since he was a small boy in Grade V."

Newcastle, Sept. 25th, 1955

Dear Jessie –

Your letter of the 2nd was very welcome, indeed. My reply will not amount to much, as I am a bit dizzy to-day. Once in a while, I have those attacks, besides I am quite a bit worried. The couple, Rev. and Mrs. Estabrooks, with whom I have boarded for four years, are leaving Newcastle on Oct. 15th, so I have to move out.

An old friend and former pupil has consented to take me. Her family is gone so she takes a few lodgers.

Once again, Margaret had to move to another place. It seems her entire adulthood consisted of moving here and there.

Her home, which belonged to her grandfather, is the house where I first boarded when I came to Newcastle to teach 64 years ago. Your mother and father called there, I think on the day they were married. They had to come to town by horse and sleigh to be married. The horse ran away, and I was thrown out, caught in the reins and dragged a distance, and hurt my arm. Your dad hurt his knee. The best man and your mother had a quiet horse, one belonging to your Uncle Ed. What a history! It makes me sad to recall the old days, and the "good-bys".

I was sorry, indeed, to hear of Etta's operation, and other afflictions. I have written to her. I had a letter from Faye since she was up to see her. She said Etta was quite discouraged. I am glad Jess is feeling better.

Sunday is a long day. I am not able to go to church now, as I cannot hear a word, even with an "aid".

Eastern USA and Canada are having hurricanes. They all have names of <u>women</u>. Not yet have they come to Margaret. When they do, they will be <u>fierce</u>.

As Margaret aged, an increasing number of her friends and family were dying or becoming ill. Her life had become narrower because of her hearing loss too. However, she still retained her sense of humor and kept up on current events.

The last one was called "Janet" - pretty bad down south.

We are sorry to hear of President Eisenhower's illness. Hope he will recover. Men like him are scarce - Republican or Democrat.

My niece's husband, who works in town called for me last week, and took me up for a short visit. I had dinner and supper with his wife, Jean, and her mother, widow of your Uncle Robert Dunnet. I enjoyed myself ever so much - Jean has two children, David, who will soon be 11, and Ruthie, who is almost 6. They live in Whitneyville. They did not see Bill and Faye, as they were living in Moncton 100 miles away. Hope you are well. Don't work too hard. Love, Aunt Margaret

Hurricane Janet was one of the strongest Atlantic hurricanes on record. It was the first Category 5 hurricane to make landfall on a continent instead of an island, and it was responsible for over a thousand deaths.

598 Brunswick St. Fredericton

March 5th, 1957

Dear Jessie –

Many thanks for birthday greetings and enclosed gift. What a good-looking group – the grandmother especially! Ethel Whitney thought you looked so young. Yes, she is a lovely person. Well why not! Her father and your Grandmother Dunnet were first cousins. Figure it out! I am looking forward to meeting her when she *arrives home in Whitneyville. She wrote me a bit about her visits, and I had a letter from the Scottish cousin in Vancouver. She writes me occasionally. I was the first Canadian cousin she met when she landed at the airport in Montreal. She flew from Scotland to Vancouver. I went out to the airport. When I met her and asked if she was "Jenny McAuley" I wish you could have seen her face when I told her I was Cousin Margaret. Her mother was Margaret Dunnet (McAuley).*

Margaret had just celebrated her ninety-first birthday, as she wrote this letter. Even at ninety-one, Margaret wrote to and received greetings, gifts, and letters from many people.

I am beginning to be a bit homesick for Newcastle. I had a wonderful celebration yesterday. Among my gifts were a dozen American Beauty roses, and a bouquet of mixed flowers. The roses came from Bertha (Whitney) Emerson in Maine. She ordered them through the florist in Houlton, Maine. Quite a number of cards contained money and postage stamps.

I shall be glad to get home just as soon as my friend in Newcastle gets better. She had promised to take me. My friend here is very kind indeed. I have a comfortable room on the first floor, breakfast in my room, etc.

The weather continues very cold, with lots of snow.

Hope your back is better. I have not much faith in osteopaths. I took months treatment in Boston - wasted money. I hurt my spine. Hope you will be benefited.

Heaps of love

Aunt Margaret

Newcastle is now called Miramichi, same as the river that flows through that part of New Brunswick.

This was the last letter, in Jessie's collection, from Aunt Margaret, and June had none after this date either. Margaret would live another year and three months. Her handwriting was still neat and legible, and her grammar and spelling were correct and proper.

Chapter 8

Jessie's grandchildren continued to write to her as they became teenagers. The kids spoke of friends, school activities, money matters, and more. The girls often wrote about clothes because Jessie was working in a dress shop and often gave them clothing as gifts. It is obvious, from reading these, that Jessie played a major role in their lives even in these teen years when peers seem to become more important than family. This first letter is from Glenda.

July 11, 1957

Dear Grandma,

How are you? I hope you are fine. Are you enjoying our wonderful rain? Doesn't it about make you mad? I wish it would get hot and stay that way for a while.

It seems funny to write. If my writing is a little scribbly, it is because my hand is a little stiff.

Thank you for the birthday present and card. I really was surprised to get it because I considered my bathing suit my birthday present. Also, my jacket.

I just got back from a 4-H swimming party. Our 4-H club had our recreational meeting out at Lake Isabelle on the other side of Shelton.

I suppose Mom told you about all our berries and fish. I picked about two buckets of berries.

> This morning Dad and I went to town. I drove in and back. We did mom's shopping for her while she stayed home and made some little wild blackberry jam. It sure is good.
>
> I got 9 dollars for my birthday and those two silk scarves from you & my bathing suit and jacket.
>
> You should have seen my birthday cake. Auntie Doris was going to buy a cake at Port Angeles but she forgot it so they put frosting between graham crackers and stuck a half of marshmallow on top and then they put a candle in the marshmallow. They also had some marshmallow on some cookies with candles in them. They

This morning Dad and I went to town. I drove in and back. We did Mom's shopping for her while she stayed home and made some little blackberry jam. It sure is good.

I got 9 dollars for my birthday and those two silk scarves from you and my bathing suit and jacket.

You should have seen my birthday cake. Auntie Doris was going to buy a cake at Port Angeles but she forgot it so they put frosting between 2 graham crackers and stuck a half marshmallow on top and then they put a candle in the marshmallow. They also had some marshmallows on some cookies with candles in them. They were real cute. It was hard to blow out 17 candles though because they were spread out so far. The wind put some out though so it wasn't too difficult.

were real cute. It was hard to blo
out seventeen candles though
because they were spread out so
far. The wind put some out,
though so it wasn't too difficult.
This Sunday there is a
picnic out at Panhandle for
Mason County Builders and
Grays Harbor County Senior
members and their guests from
Yakima County Grays Harbor and
Yakima are having an exchange,
that is why Yakima County kids
will be there.
Sunday our church
is having a picnic also but
theirs is at Mason Lake. I
don't know which one I will
go to yet.
I guess I better quit as I
have to go to bed now. If I think
of anything more I will add it in

This Sunday there is a picnic out at Panhandle for Mason County Builders and Grays County Senior members and their guests from Yakima County. Grays Harbor and Yakima are having an exchange; that is why Yakima County kids will be there.

Sunday our church is having a picnic also but theirs is at Mason Lake. I don't know which one I will go to yet.

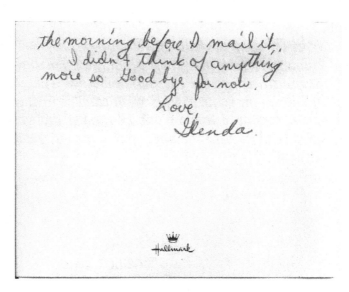

I guess I better quit as I have to go to bed now. If I think of anything more I will add it in the morning before I mail it.

I didn't think of anything more so Good bye for now.

Love,

Glenda

   This next letter was written by Pat when she was in junior high.

Dear Grandma,

Thank you so much for the sweater, slip and socks. I just love them. This is one of the pens you gave daddy. He sure keeps them to himself. But I got it away from him to write this letter.

I went bowling with Anne and Margee yesterday. It was the first time I ever bowled and I got 79. It was real fun though. I went babysitting for a while tonight but they weren't gone very long.

Well, I have two more "thank yous" to write so I better close now.

Thanks again.

Love,

Pat

Oct. 2, 1958

Dear Grandma,

Isn't this fancy paper? Thanks a lot for the money and card. I got material for a skirt and money for a sweater from Mom & Daddy. Jean gave me a bottle of perfume. It's really rare too.

How much do I owe on that red skirt? I meant to pay you right away but I just never got around to it. I'll send you $10.00 and pay the rest next time I see you because I don't know how much I owe. I'm sorry I waited so long, but I kept forgetting though.

Mom said to tell you she didn't invite Forthsythes (??Spelling??) up Sun. because she's working and can't manage it. She said to tell you and Glenda to come any way.

Well I'll see you then. I don't have time to write any more.

Thanks again. Love, Pat

Bill's daughter Pat wrote this letter on her fifteenth birthday. Glenda attended her first two years of college at Skagit Valley College and lived with Jessie, so it would have been natural for her to come with Jessie for Sunday dinner. The Pulvers and Jessie had Sunday dinner together most weeks while the kids were growing up. When they were younger, the Pulvers usually drove down to Burlington, but as the kids became teenagers, it was more likely that Jessie would join them in Bellingham.

Dear Grandma,

I just got home from school and I should be doing my homework, but I'm not. I got an "A" on a history test today, an "A" on an algebra test Friday, and an "A-" on an English test a few days ago. So you can see I've been studying.

My favorite class this year is Journalism. We write stories for the school paper & get ads too. That's why I was down town during school last week when I saw you. It's really a ball.

I have cooking this year too & it's a lot of fun. We made cinnamon rolls last week.

When we play Burlington Fri. we're going to win. We lost to Mt. Vernon last week. Our team made two touchdowns though.

You know Shirley Askildson, that friend of mine? She's running for "What a sho" queen. I know she'll get it too. She's so cute. A friend of Jean's is running too but she won't get it because she's too fat.

The What-a-Sho was a talent show at Bellingham High School that had elected royalty. Shirley did go on to become the junior class royalty (and Jean's friend was probably not the least bit fat).

Mom said I can get my permit Friday. She's going to pick me up from school. Isn't that rare?

Did you hear about that ex-Bellingham boy that killed his dad & sister & then himself? He's the same age as Jo & we knew him when he lived here. Don used to play with him and Jo was in some of his classes. I think they moved this summer.

Jean got a type-writer today. It's really neat – a portable, green one.

I have to go to a Sunday school teachers meeting tonight. I really like teaching. It's so much fun.

Tomorrow I have to go to the library, Wed. is Y-teens and Fri. the game. I'm never home any more.

Before the games each week someone has a dinner and about 8-10 kids go. It's really fun. I think we're coming here next week.

I better get busy and help Mom with dinner now. Don't laugh – I do help sometimes.

Write soon.

Love, Pat

Back in the '60s, teenagers got their driving permits when they turned sixteen rather than at fifteen the way they do now. In Bellingham, the kids often used the word "rare" to describe something they thought was good. This seemed to be a short-term fad.

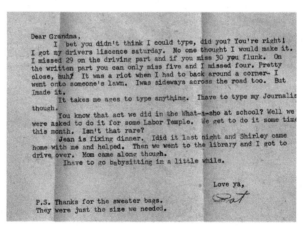

Dear Grandma,

I bet you didn't think I could type, did you? You're right! I got my driver's license Saturday. No one thought I would make it. I missed 29 on the driving part and if you miss 30 you flunk. On the written part you can only miss five and I missed four. Pretty close, huh? It was a riot when I had to back around a corner – I went onto someone's lawn. I was sideways across the road too. But I made it.

It takes me ages to type anything. I have to type my Journalism though.

You know that act we did in the What-a-Sho at school? Well we were asked to do it for some Labor Temple. We get to do it sometime this month. Isn't that rare?

Jean is fixing dinner. I did it last night and Shirley came home with me and helped. Then we went to the library and I got to drive over. Mom came along though.

I have to go babysitting in a little while.

Love ya, Pat

P.S. Thanks for the sweater bags. They were just the size we needed.

The Pulver girls still laugh about the sweater bags they were expected to keep their sweaters in, and how they were always reminded how neatly their cousin Glenda folded her sweaters and how she <u>always</u> put them in the drawers in their bags. Pat, Jean, and Jo were somewhat careless with theirs, and the sweaters did not always find their way into bags and then drawers.

Jessie's grandniece, Patty Harlow (Rosamond's granddaughter), grew up in Portland, Oregon, but she visited Jessie occasionally and sent her this note on the back of a birthday card in 1961.

August 4, 1961

Dear Aunt Jessie,

How are you? We are all fine down here.

It's been hot here. Yesterday it got close to 100 degrees.

I wish I could come up there this summer. But I doubt it.

Just think you'll be about 30 this month.

Well, I have to go. Tell everyone hello.

And {Happy} {Birthday}

Love,

Patty

Dear Grandma,   *Saturday*

Isn't this paper hideous? I got it last summer and I guess I better use it up. I wrote you a letter about a week ago, but I didn't have time to finish it and mail it. All day today I've been painting my room. It really looks nice though.

I got your letter a couple days ago. Thanks for the picture – it was good of Maverick. I was standing like a freak or something.

Jo went skiing today. Mom wouldn't let me because she says I'm not well. That's a laugh. I have to stay home tonight too because she says I have to get my rest.

I got to go last week though and it was really a ball. It's so expensive though. It cost $5.50 so I can't afford it very often.

Maverick was one of the horses owned by the Pulvers.

I don't think I've thanked you for the Christmas presents yet. I really did like everything though. I wear the nightgown all the time.

Those pencils really caused a riot at school. Everybody wants one.

Susan Duzenbery is up for the weekend. I think Jeff is too but neither one of them is staying here. Susan has been here all day though.

I've been working so hard on my studying lately. We've had finals and everything all at once. I think I'll probably get about same as I did last qtr. That was two A's & 3 B's. If I could bring one B up to an A I could make the honor roll.

I better go now. I'll see you.

Love, Pat

The pencils she referred to were a stocking gift, at Christmas, from Jessie to all her grandchildren. Instead of having their names printed on them, the pencils said, "stolen from" beside their names. Their friends thought it was fun to have a pencil saying it was stolen from a Pulver or Gee kid.

Steve Pulver was serving in the Coast Guard at this time and was stationed on an Icebreaker called the *Northwind*. He wrote the following letter while on duty on the ship.

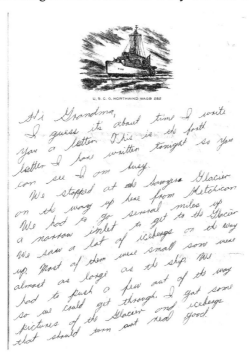

Hi Grandma,

I guess it's about time I write you a letter. This is the fourth letter I have written tonight so you can see I am busy.

We stopped at the Sawyer Glacier on the way up here from Ketchikan. We had to go several miles up a narrow inlet to get to the Glacier. We saw a lot of icebergs on the way up. Most of them were small some were almost as large as the ship. We had to push a few out of the way so we could get through. I got some pictures of the Glacier and icebergs that should turn out real good.

The Sawyer Glacier is located near Juneau, Alaska.

The icebergs are a real pretty blue. I found a post card that showed the Glacier that I'll send you. This town sure seems small for the capitol of the largest state in the union.

Juneau and Douglas, a small town across the bay, have a population of about 9,000. The streets are real narrow and the buildings are old. The cars here are all banged up. It seemed like almost all of them had at least one fender banged up.

We are leaving Sat. for Kodiak. I don't know when our E.T.A. (estimated time of arrival) is.

Tomorrow I am going on a sightseeing tour around Juneau and out to Mendenhall Glacier. It's not too far from here.

There is some real pretty country around here. If you ever get a chance you should see it. I have about 10 rolls of film with me and will probably buy more so you will see some of it.

Well, had better quit for now.

Love, Steve

Meanwhile, Pat was in college at Washington State University in Pullman, Washington. Vera went over for Mom's weekend, and Jessie had given her pajamas and a robe for the trip. Vera wrote the following letter of thanks.

Dear Mom,

I had a wonderful time with Pat. We both love the P.J.'s and robe & thanks again. We were so busy over there. The time went so fast.

Can you come for dinner Sun.? I think Bill will be plowing. Would you like to come up and go to church with us girls? 10:45.

Must mail this. Jo is in the store.

Love,

Vera & all

Bring Auntie Mern or Aunt Etta along if you like.

Mern was Jessie's sister-in-law, Rude's sister. The Pulver in-laws were always a part of Jessie's life.

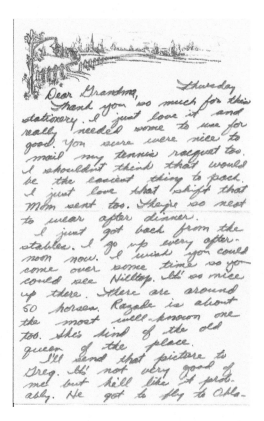

Dear Grandma, Thursday

Thank you so much for this stationary. I just love it and really needed some to use for good. You sure were nice to mail my tennis racquet. I shouldn't think that would be the easiest thing to pack. I just love that shift that Mom sent too. They're so neat to wear after dinner.

I just got back from the stables. I go up every afternoon now. I wish you could come over some time so you could see Hilltop. It's so nice up there. There are around 50 horses. Razade is about the most well-known one too. She's kind of the old queen of the place.

I'll send that picture to Greg. It's not very good of me but he'll like it probably. He got to fly to Oklahoma.

During Pat's time at WSU, there was a horse-breeding program in place, and since the horses needed to be exercised, students were assigned horses if they asked. Pat and her room-mate, Ann Marie, had horses and rode them almost daily.

Greg was Pat's high school boyfriend and her future husband. He had just joined the National Guard and was stationed in Fort Sill, Oklahoma. Greg and Pat recently celebrated their fiftieth anniversary.

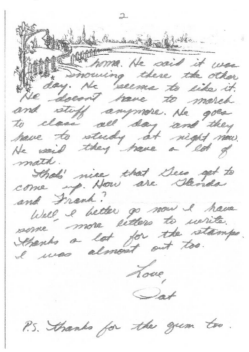

He said it was snowing there the other day. He seems to like it. He doesn't have to march and stuff anymore. He goes to class all day and they have to study at night now. He said they have a lot of math.

That's nice that Gees get to come up. How are Glenda and Frank?

Well, I better go now I have some more letters to write. Thanks a lot for the stamps. I was almost out too.

Love,

Pat

P.S. Thanks for the gum too.

By this time, Glenda had married Frank Nelson, and they lived in Skagit County, near Jessie. They later moved to Eastern Washington. They celebrated fifty years of marriage before Frank died in 2014.

The next letter was written to Jessie by Don Pulver, who was 12 years of age at the time. He reports on the happenings of two of his older sisters, Jean and Pat, and tells Jessie what he and his friends were up to.

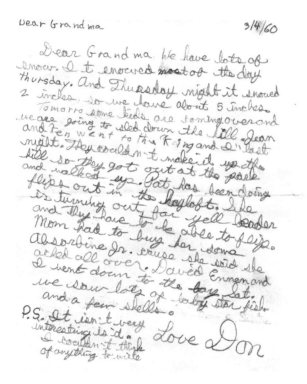

Dear Grandma   *3/4/60*

We have lots of snow. It snowed most of the day Thursday. And Thursday night it snowed 2 inches, so we have about 5 inches. Tomorrow some kids are coming over and we are going to sled down the hill. Jean and Ken went to the "King and I" last night. They couldn't make it up the hill so they got out at the park and walked up. Pat has been doing flips out in the hayloft. She is turning out for yell leader and they have to be able to flip. Mom had to buy her some Absorbine Jr. cause she said she ached all over.

David Ennen and I went down to the bay Sat. We saw lots of baby star fish and a few shells.

Love, Don

P.S. It isn't very interesting is it? I couldn't think of anything to write.

Vera was well known for thinking Absorbine Jr., a pain reliever, could cure most anything. Even Jessie joked that Vera brushed her teeth with Absorbine Jr.

Jessie had a close relationship with all of her grandchildren – knowing the favorite foods of each of them and serving those often. Steve, for example, got green Jell-O with grated carrots and chunks of celery in it. Even great-granddaughter Heidi was served one of her favorites – canned grapefruit sections – when she visited Jessie's house.

Chapter 9

In the 1970's Jessie began getting letters from her great-grandchildren. Christine and Robert Finney are the children of Jean Pulver Finney and her husband, Rick. Tyler, Aaron, and Heidi are the children of Patricia Pulver Fitzgerald and her husband, Greg. The great-grandchildren, beginning with Glenda's first son, Terry, always called Jessie "Grandmother."

Dear Grandmother,

How are you doing? I am fine. Yesterday I rode my horse to school. I rode with my friend named Shawn. We rode to some peoples house and tied them up at some trees.

We are going to visit our friends that live in Seattle on Monday.

It will be spring vacation. It's raining today, so I can't ride Misty today. (Misty's my horse). I hope you get well soon.

Love Christine

Jean's family lived on Lummi Island, which is one of the San Juan Islands off the coast of Washington. They had acreage and a few animals. Rick worked in the summers as a commercial fisherman.

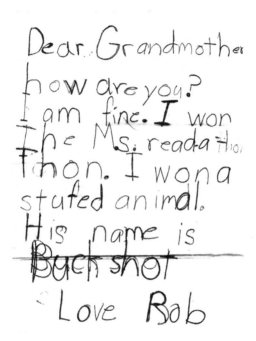

Dear Grandmother,

How are you? I am fine. I won the M.S. Read-a-thon. I won a stuffed animal. His name is Buckshot.

Love Rob

Teresa Pulver, Steve and Nola's daughter, sent this picture to Jessie when she was about five or six years old. The girl is saying, "Teresa said I can jump," and the boy is saying, "Robby said I can fall."

The rings that Teresa has drawn herself hanging from were originally used by Bill and June Pulver, then Bill and Vera Pulver's five children, and then Rita and Teresa Pulver. They are currently in Steve's shop.

Dear Grandmother

Happy Birthday. Rita got a new shirt today. It says in the front Mt. Rainier Nat'l Park. On the back it says go climb the mountain. We spent the night at Lodge Pole Campground. Today we are spending the night at Big Creek Campground. I got a new shirt. It says Mount Rainier and has a fawn on it. I decided to save for the Lynden Fair.

Love Teresa

Teresa refers to her sister, Rita, in this letter. Rita was born in 1967 and Teresa in 1969. They lived near Ferndale, Washington at this time.

Dear Grandmother
Hows your arm?
Saturday we
went out in
Grandpa's boat.
and we spent the
night at Succa.
and Sunday we
went to a wheel
and keel por luck.
(over)

Sun. 15
Easter day

Dear Grandmother,
How have you been latley?
I got this new stationary from the Easter Bunny. This morning we hunted Easter eggs. It was fun!
Yesterday Mom & I went for a bike ride. Down to the store. When we got home it started pouring down hail! They were huge hail balls! (hail balls, ha ha)
I hope we can go & see you soon!
Today is our last day of Spring vacation. I don't want to go back to school!
Tonight we are having a turkey dinner. (For easter)
P.S. I hope to see

Sun. 15 Easter day

Dear Grandmother,

How have you been lately?

I got this new stationary from the Easter Bunny. This morning we hunted Easter eggs. It was fun!

Yesterday Mom & I went for a bike ride. Down to the store. When we got home it started pouring down hail! They were huge hail balls! (hail balls, ha ha)

I hope we can go & see you soon!

Today is our last day of Spring vacation. I don't want to go back to school!

Tonight we are having a turkey dinner. (For Easter)

Love Christine   P.S. I hope to see you soon!

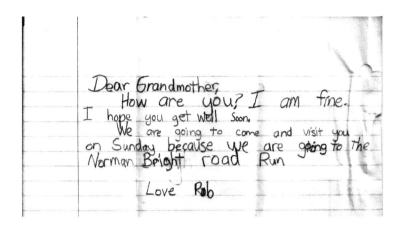

Dear Grandmother,

How are you? I am fine. I hope you get well soon.

We are going to come and visit you on Sunday because we are going to the Norman Bright road Run.

Love Rob

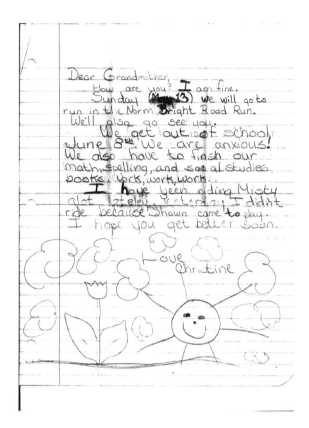

Dear Grandmother,

How are you? I am fine.

Sunday (May 13) we will go to run in the Norm Bright Road Run. We'll also go see you.

We get out of school June 8th. We are anxious! We also have to finish our math, spelling, and social studies books. Work, work, work.

I have been riding Misty a lot lately. Yesterday I didn't ride because Shawn came to play. I hope you get better soon.

Love

Christine

Christine is shown here on her horse, Misty, with her cousin
Tyler Fitzgerald.

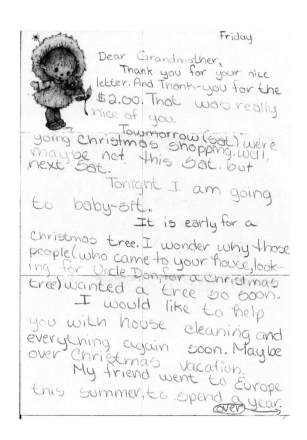

Friday

Dear Grandmother,

Thank you for your nice letter. And thank-you for the $2.00. That was really nice of you.

Tomorrow (Sat.) we're going Christmas shopping. Well, maybe not this Sat. but next Sat.

Tonight I am going to baby-sit.

It is early for a Christmas tree. I wonder why those people (who came to your house, looking for Uncle Don, for a Christmas tree) wanted a tree so soon.

I would like to help you with house cleaning and everything again soon. Maybe over Christmas vacation.

My friend went to Europe this summer, to spend a year.

The Christmas trees that Christine referred to were grown by Bill Pulver as a source of retirement income. Bill and Vera lived on about eight acres of land on the Old Samish Road in Bellingham. Don and his wife, Joyce, lived across the street with their children, Jon, Katie, and Mark. Jessie, at this point, had moved into a smaller place on Don's property, so they were all near one another.

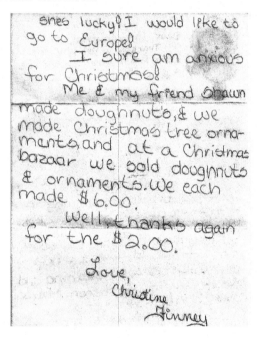

She's lucky! I would like to go to Europe!

I sure am anxious for Christmas!

Me & my friend Shawn made doughnut's, & we made Christmas tree ornaments, and at a Christmas bazaar we sold doughnuts & ornaments. We each made $6.00.

Well, thanks again for the $2.00

Love,

Christine Finney

Bill was present to help June and Glen celebrate their fiftieth wedding anniversary. They lived in Olympia at the time, and Bill was in Bellingham. Vera had died in 1978.

June Pulver Gee and Bill Pulver.

A very young Tyler Fitzgerald, Pat's son, wrote this letter to his great-grandmother stating, "Grandmother Tyler loves you."

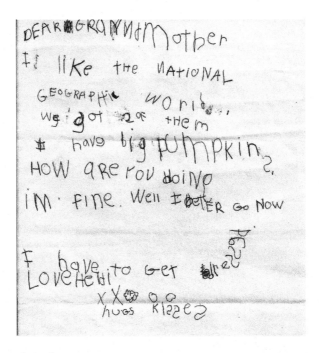

Dear Grandmother

I like the National Geographic World. We got 2 of them. I have big pumpkins. How are you doing I'm fine. Well I better go now

I have to get dressed.

Love Heidi

XX   OO

Hugs kisses

National Geographic World, a children's magazine, was a gift to the Fitzgerald children from Jessie.

Dear Grandmother.

Thank you for the two dollars. I got a chek for five dollars and I put the money together and I had enough to buy something. So I bought a swimming suit. I lost my two front teeth. I'm going to watch the apple blossom parade right now

Love Heidi

It seems Jessie's standard gift to her great-grandchildren for their birthdays was $2.00. She also included a letter and a birthday card. Through letters, Jessie enjoyed a close relationship with these great-grandchildren. The Fitzgerald children lived in Wenatchee, a three- to four-hour drive from her home in Burlington, and later Bellingham, so she saw them less frequently than those who lived closer.

Hi Grandmother

How are you? I'm fine. Happy Mothers Day!!

Heidi Fitzgerald

Hope you have a nice mother's day

Aaron

P.S. Hope you like the book

Happy Mother's day!

Love Tyler

The three Fitzgerald children each wrote a little note in a Mother's Day card.

Tyler and Aaron Fitzgerald   Heidi Fitzgerald

Friday

Dear Grandmother,

How are you? I'm O.K.

I'm sure glad today is Friday! I write Rita letters & give them to her at school. We don't see each other very much.

Rob has a friend over to spend the night.

Ferndale started to flood today. Rain, rain, rain! The school yard has mud puddles all over.

I'm getting sick of the rain!

Tonight we are having encheladas. My favorite.

Love,

Christine

Rita is Christine's cousin and the oldest daughter of Steve and his wife, Nola. She and Christine were born just a month apart and, at this point, were at the same school in Ferndale. Beginning in sixth grade, Christine went to Vista Middle School in Ferndale rather than the small one-room school on Lummi Island. Rob went to Skyline Elementary in Ferndale for fifth grade, because there were no other kids his age on the island, and attended middle school the next year.

Dear Grandmother,

How does your arm feel? I liked the card you sent me! I got four new bantam hens so now I have eight hens and One rooster. I can't wait till my birthday! Thank you for the two dollars. Christine got fifth in the fifty yd. dash at Arco Jesse Owens Games

Love Rob

Jessie had broken her arm, a sign of the osteoporosis she suffered from in her later years.

6-27-79
2001 N. Nugent Rd.
Lummi Island, Wa.
98262

Dear Grandmother,

How are you? I am fine.

In a week (from yesterday) I am going to camp. My friends Shawn and Kim are going, too! I'm excited. I've never gone to camp!

Day before yesterday Shawn and I babysitted from noon to 10:00 p.m. Tonight we will sit from 6:30-12:30 p.m. We babysit together for some people named the Lukes.

Yesterday my friends, Jane, Nancy and Shawn went swimming at *a lake that's on the Mountain (Lummi Mt.). We had a good time.*

Today I was going to give Misty a bath but it doesn't seem warm enough. Rob had a good birthday.

Christine is referring to a 4-H camp she attended that year on Whidbey Island, a large island two hours south of Lummi.

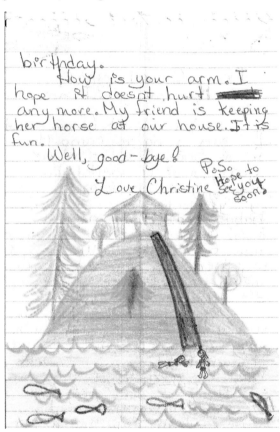

How is your arm. I hope it doesn't hurt any more. My friend is keeping her horse at our house. It is fun.

Well, good-bye!

Love Christine

P.S. Hope to see you soon!

The Finney family – Jean, Christine, Rob, and Rick

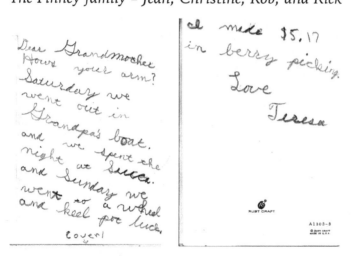

Dear Grandmother

How's your arm? Saturday we went out in Grandpa's boat, and we spent the night on Sucia. And Sunday we went to a Wheel and Keel pot luck. I made $5.17 in berry picking.

Love Teresa

Teresa is the younger daughter of Steve Pulver and his wife, Nola. Bill and Vera did a lot of boating in the San Juan Islands, and the kids and grandchildren were included in many of these adventures. Sucia is a publicly owned island. Wheel and Keel was a boating club that Bill and Vera belonged to for many years. Teresa refers to berry picking. Growing up in Whatcom County, strawberry picking was a part of the lives of generations of local children.

Teresa Lynn Pulver

Dear Grandmother

How are you? I'm fine.

We stopped by but you were gone. Did you get mom's note? After we stopped by we went to the new park. Rita and I roller skated.

P.S. Sorry I didn't write much but I didn't have time.

It is presumed that Teresa left this note on Jessie's door after they found she wasn't home because on the reverse side is a note from a friend in Burlington who had also stopped by and found Jessie not home.

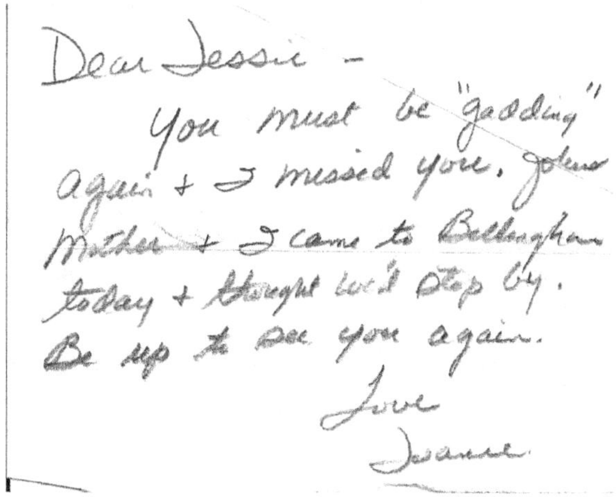

Dear Jessie -
You must be "gadding"
again & I missed you. John's
Mother & I came to Bellingham
today & thought we'd stop by.
Be up to see you again.
Love
Joanie

Dear Jessie -

You must be "gadding" again & I missed you. John's mother & I came to Bellingham today & thought we'd stop by. Be up to see you again.

Love Joanie

Dear Grandmother,

Hi! This week is Spring vacation for us expect we have to go to school Monday & Tuesday to make up for the days we missed because of the snow. This week (Wednesday & Thursday) Rita and I are going to stay with our friends at their cabin then when we get home we are going camping probably at the river.

Love,

Teresa

In Whatcom County it took very little snow to close down the schools, but the days did have to be made up so that the full 180 days would be spent in school.

Chapter 10

Jessie Whitney Pulver was born in 1896, 120 years ago. Because she saved many of the letters she received over her lifetime, she left a treasure, not measured in dollars but in something intangible, to her family and to others. These letters give us a glimpse into the lives of Jessie's grandmother, her parents, her aunt, her children, grandchildren, and even great-grandchildren. They take us from the early twentieth century into the 1980's.

Margaret was the most prolific of the writers, and she was able to describe the world around her and the changes she saw -- history in the making -- while she also spoke of day-to-day family life. One of Margaret's concerns was that when she died there would no longer be a connection between relatives of her sister Anna Rose Whitney, in Burlington, Washington, and the majority of the family who lived in New Brunswick, Canada.

In fact, there was no contact for many years after Margaret died. However, the technology of the late twentieth and early twenty-first centuries changed everything. It became possible to trace one's family through Internet searches, Ancestry.com, and software such as Family Tree Maker.

I am Patricia Pulver Fitzgerald, the author of this book and Jessie's granddaughter. Through the pursuit of family history and social media, I was able to connect with Ruth Creighton Somers and her brother David, Margaret's grandniece and nephew. Both of them were mentioned frequently in Margaret's letters to Jessie. They are the children of Jean Dunnet and the grandchildren of Robert Dunnet, my great-grandmother's brother.

In June of 2015, I took my sixteen-year-old granddaughter, Cameron Kunz, child of my daughter, Heidi Fitzgerald Kunz and her husband Craig, to New Brunswick to visit these family members and to see the places where her great-great-great-

great grandmother, Jane Forsyth Dunnet, lived her life. She met Jean and David and got to know these distant cousins and to appreciate their connection to the past that she shares with them. Jean lives in the home of her grandparents, Robert Forsyth Dunnet and Ruth Mutch Dunnet. Margaret had visited this house frequently, so we were able to walk through, eat, and sleep in the house where Margaret and her brother had spent time.

Every family has connections to people from the past, and it is a thrill to find out about those people, who they were, who they loved, what they did to earn a living, their connections to other family members, and how they viewed the world of their time.

CPSIA information can be obtained
at www.ICGtesting.com
Printed in the USA
LVOW05s0453190216

475805LV00027B/491/P